First World War
and Army of Occupation
War Diary
France, Belgium and Germany

16 DIVISION
49 Infantry Brigade,
Brigade Machine Gun Company
(1 May 1916 - 28 February 1918)
and Brigade Trench Mortar Battery
(10 November 1914 - 28 December)

WO95/1979/5

The Naval & Military Press Ltd
www.nmarchive.com
Published in association with The National Archives

Published by

The Naval & Military Press Ltd

Unit 10 Ridgewood Industrial Park,

Uckfield, East Sussex,

TN22 5QE England

Tel: +44 (0) 1825 749494

www.naval-military-press.com

www.nmarchive.com

This diary has been reprinted in facsimile from the original. Any imperfections are inevitably reproduced and the quality may fall short of modern type and cartographic standards.

© Crown Copyright
Images reproduced by permission of The National Archives, London, England, 2015.

Contents

Document type	Place/Title	Date From	Date To
Heading	1979/5 Brigade Machine Gun Company. May 1916-1918 Feb		
Heading	16th Division 49th Infy Bde 49th Machine Gun Coy. May 1916-Feb 1918		
War Diary	Noeux Les Mines	01/05/1916	02/05/1916
War Diary	Noeux Les Mines Trenches Hulluch Sector	03/05/1916	03/05/1916
War Diary	Trenches Hulluch Sector	04/05/1916	06/05/1916
War Diary	Noeux Les Mines	06/05/1916	17/05/1916
War Diary	Noeux Les Mines Trenches Loos Sector.	18/05/1916	18/05/1916
War Diary	Trenches Loos	19/05/1916	30/05/1916
War Diary	Loos	01/06/1916	08/06/1916
War Diary	14 Bis	09/06/1916	25/06/1916
Heading	War Diary 49 Machine Gun Company 1st. July To 31st. July 1916. Volume No. 3		
War Diary	Loos	01/07/1916	19/07/1916
War Diary	Noeux	20/07/1916	20/07/1916
War Diary	Hulluch	21/07/1916	23/07/1916
War Diary	Noeux	24/07/1916	29/07/1916
War Diary	14 Bis	30/07/1916	31/07/1916
Heading	War Diary 49th Machine Gun Company Month Of August, 1916. Volume:-5		
War Diary	14 Bis	01/08/1916	23/08/1916
War Diary	Noeux-Les-Mines	24/08/1916	26/08/1916
War Diary	Marles-les-Mines	27/08/1916	29/08/1916
War Diary	Sailly-le-Sec	30/08/1916	31/08/1916
Heading	War Diary 49th Machine Gun Company For Month Of September, 1916.		
War Diary	Rest at Gibralter	01/09/1916	03/09/1916
War Diary	Billon Farm	04/09/1916	04/09/1916
War Diary	In The Field	05/09/1916	07/09/1916
War Diary	Resting at Billon Farm	08/09/1916	08/09/1916
War Diary	In The Field	09/09/1916	11/09/1916
War Diary	Sailly Le Sec	12/09/1916	18/09/1916
War Diary	Wanel	19/09/1916	21/09/1916
War Diary	Kemmel	22/09/1916	30/09/1916
Operation(al) Order(s)	49th Machine Gun Company. Report On Operations 8th to 10th September 1916	08/09/1916	08/09/1916
War Diary	Kemmel	01/10/1916	30/11/1916
Heading	War Diary For Month Of December. 1916 Volume 9 49 Machine Gun Company.		
War Diary	Kemmel	01/12/1916	31/12/1916
Heading	War Diary for month of January, 1917. Volume 10 49th Machine Gun Company.		
War Diary	Wytschaete Sector	01/01/1917	31/01/1917
Heading	War Diary. For Month Of February, 1917. Volume 11 Unit:- 49th Machine Gun Company		
War Diary	Wytschaete Sector	01/02/1917	28/02/1917
Heading	War Diary For Month Of March, 1917. Volume 12 Unit:- 49th Machine Gun Company		
War Diary	Wytschaete Sector	01/03/1917	17/03/1917

War Diary	Vierstraat Sector	18/03/1917	31/03/1917
Heading	War Diary For Month Of April, 1917. Volume:- 13 Unit:- 49th Machine Gun Company		
War Diary	Vierstraat Sector	01/04/1917	12/04/1917
War Diary	Recques Area	13/04/1917	30/04/1917
Heading	War Diary Volume:-14 For Month Of May, 1917. Unit:- 49th Machine Gun Company		
War Diary	Diependaal Sector	01/05/1917	10/05/1917
War Diary	Vierstraat Sector	10/05/1917	31/05/1917
War Diary	Vierstraat Sector	18/05/1917	18/05/1917
Heading	War Diary. For Month Of June, 1917. Volume:- 15. Unit:- 49th Machine Gun Company		
War Diary	Klondyke Fm.	01/06/1917	02/06/1917
War Diary	In the line Vierstraat Area	03/06/1917	10/06/1917
War Diary	Locre Area	11/06/1917	13/06/1917
War Diary	Merris	14/06/1917	16/06/1917
War Diary	Locre Area	17/06/1917	18/06/1917
War Diary	Merris	19/06/1917	21/06/1917
War Diary	Eecke Area	22/06/1917	22/06/1917
War Diary	Buysscheure Area	23/06/1917	24/06/1917
War Diary	Buysscheure	25/06/1917	30/06/1917
Miscellaneous			
Miscellaneous	Report On Operations	07/06/1917	07/06/1917
Miscellaneous	Report On Operations Of M.G at Mauveline From The Time Of Leaving The Hospice Till Being Relieve By The 33rd M.G. Coy.		
Miscellaneous	Report On Operations "B" Sect	07/06/1917	07/06/1917
Miscellaneous	Report On Operations "C" Sect	07/06/1917	07/06/1917
Miscellaneous	Report On Operations	07/06/1917	07/06/1917
Heading	War Diary. For Month Of July, 1917. Volume:- 16 Unit:- 49th Machine Gun Company		
Miscellaneous	War Diary Of The 49th Company, Machine Gun Corps. From 1st July 1917-31st July 1917 (Inclusive)		
War Diary	Tatinghem Ref. Map Belgium Hazebrouck 5 A 1/100,000	01/07/1917	09/07/1917
War Diary	Winnizeele Ref. Map Belgium Hazebrouck 5 A 1/100,000	10/07/1917	26/07/1917
War Diary	Watou (area No. 2) Ref. Map Belgium Hazebrouck 5 A 1/100,000	27/07/1917	31/07/1917
Heading	War Diary. For Month Of August, 1917. Volume 17 Unit 49th Machine Gun Company.		
Heading	War Diary Of The 49th Machine Gun Company For August 1917		
War Diary	Bedouin Camp Ref Sheet 28 N. W. G 6 B 60.30	01/08/1917	01/08/1917
War Diary	Vlamertinghe	02/08/1917	02/08/1917
War Diary	Bedouin Camp	03/08/1917	03/08/1917
War Diary	Mill Cot.	04/08/1917	10/08/1917
War Diary	Coy Hdq H 16 D 5.4	11/08/1917	13/08/1917
War Diary	Mill Cot	14/08/1917	17/08/1917
War Diary	Coy Hdq H 16 D 5.4 Sheet 28 N.W.	18/08/1917	18/08/1917
War Diary	Coy Hdq K 17 B 3.4	19/08/1917	19/08/1917
War Diary	Coy Hdq. Godewaelweld	20/08/1917	31/08/1917
Heading	War Diary. For Month Of September, 1917. Volume 18 Unit:- M.G.C. 49th Machine Gun Coy.		
War Diary	Moyenneville	01/09/1917	30/09/1917

Heading	War Diary For Month Of October, 1917. Unit 49th Machine Gun Company Volume Number 19		
Miscellaneous	Confidential War Diary Of The 49th Machine Gun Coy For October 1917		
War Diary	Moyenneville Map Reference Bullecourt 51 B.S. W. 4	01/10/1917	31/10/1917
Heading	War Diary For Month Of November. 1917. Volume:- 20 Unit:- 49th Machine Gun Company		
Miscellaneous	War Diary Of The 49th Machine Gun Coy For November 1917		
War Diary	Moyenneville Map Reference Bullecourt 51 B S W 4	01/11/1917	30/11/1917
Operation(al) Order(s)	49th Machine Gun Company Operation Order No. 1	18/11/1917	13/11/1917
Miscellaneous	Appendix "A" Group No. 8		
Heading	War Diary, For Month Of December, 1917. Volume:- 21 Unit:- 49th Machine Gun Company M.G.C.		
Miscellaneous	War Diary Of The 49th Machine Gun Coy. For December 1917		
War Diary	Moyenneville	01/12/1917	01/12/1917
War Diary	Map Ref Bullecourt 51 B S W 4	01/12/1917	02/12/1917
War Diary	Map Ref Sheet 57 C 1/40,000	03/12/1917	05/12/1917
War Diary	Map Ref. Sheet 62 C 1/40,000	06/12/1917	13/12/1917
War Diary	Ephey 1.10000	14/12/1917	22/12/1917
War Diary	Map Ref Sheet 62 C 1/40,000	23/12/1917	28/12/1917
War Diary	St Emelie	29/12/1917	30/12/1917
War Diary	Ephey 1:10000	31/12/1917	31/12/1917
Heading	War Diary, For Month Of January, 1918. Volume:- 22 Unit:- 49th Machine Gun Company M.G.C.		
Miscellaneous	War Diary Of The 49th Machine Gun Company For January 1918		
War Diary	St Emelie	01/01/1918	01/01/1918
War Diary	Epehy 1.10,000	02/01/1918	02/01/1918
War Diary	Ref. Maps Lempire Special Sheet 1:10,000	03/01/1918	04/01/1918
War Diary	St Emelie	05/01/1918	05/01/1918
War Diary	Epehy 1.10,000	06/01/1918	06/01/1918
War Diary	Lempire Special Sheet 1:10,000	07/01/1918	07/01/1918
War Diary	St Emelie	08/01/1918	08/01/1918
War Diary	Epehy 1:10000	09/01/1918	09/01/1918
War Diary	Lempire Special Sheet 1:10,000	10/01/1918	10/01/1918
War Diary	St. Emelie	10/01/1918	10/01/1918
War Diary	Ephey 1.10,000	11/01/1918	11/01/1918
War Diary	Lempire Special Sheet 1.10.000 Tincourt	12/01/1918	12/01/1918
War Diary	Lempire Special Sheet 1.10,000 Tincourt. 62 C 1.40,000	13/01/1917	13/01/1917
War Diary	Tincourt.	13/01/1918	13/01/1918
War Diary	Tincourt 62C 1.40000 Special Sheet Epehy 4d.2 A	14/01/1918	14/01/1918
War Diary	Tincourt.	14/01/1918	14/01/1918
War Diary	Epehy Ad.2 A 1.10000	14/01/1918	19/01/1918
War Diary	St Emelie Lempire Special Sheet 1.100000	20/01/1918	20/01/1918
War Diary	St Emelie	21/01/1918	21/01/1918
War Diary	Epehy 1.10,000	22/01/1918	22/01/1918
War Diary	Lempire Special Sheet 1.10,000	23/01/1918	23/01/1918
Heading	War Diary Of 49th Machine Gun Company For Month Of February 1918		
War Diary	Tincourt Ref. Maps Sheet 62c N.E. 2 Special Sheet Parts Of 57 C S.E. 57 B S.F. 62 C N.E. And 62 B N. W.	01/02/1918	08/02/1918

War Diary	St. Emelie Ref. Maps Sheet 62c N.E. 2 Special Sheet Parts Of 57 C S E. 57 B S.W. 62 C N.E. And 62 B N. W.	09/02/1918	09/02/1918
War Diary	St. Emelie	10/02/1918	18/02/1918
War Diary	St. Emelie	24/01/1918	24/01/1918
War Diary	Epehy 1.10,000	24/01/1918	25/01/1918
War Diary	Lempire Special Sheet 1.10,000	25/01/1918	25/01/1918
War Diary	St Emelie	26/01/1918	26/01/1918
War Diary	Ephey 1:10,000	26/01/1918	27/01/1918
War Diary	Lempire Special Sheet 1.10,000	28/01/1918	28/01/1918
War Diary	St. Emelie	29/01/1918	29/01/1918
War Diary	Ephey 1:10,000	29/01/1918	30/01/1918
War Diary	Lempire Special Sheet 1:10,000 Tincourt	31/01/1918	31/01/1918
Miscellaneous	49th Machine Gun Coy Training Programme For Period Jan 12th To 18th 1918		
Heading	War Diary. For Month Of February, 1918. Volume:- 23 Unit:- 49th Machine Gun Compy		
War Diary	St Emelie	19/02/1918	28/02/1918
Miscellaneous	Training Programme 31.1.18 To 7.2.18 - 49th Machine Gun Coy.	31/01/1918	31/01/1918
Heading	1979/6 Brigade Trench Mortar Battery Oct 1915-Dec 1915		
Heading	16 Div 49 Bde 49 Trench Mortar Bty 1915 Oct To 1915 Dec		
War Diary	Berthen	09/11/1915	09/11/1915
War Diary	Nieppe	10/11/1914	14/11/1914
War Diary	Plug St Wood	15/11/1915	19/11/1915
War Diary	1/20000 Sheet 25 C IV. 1329a 33	26/10/1915	30/10/1915
War Diary	Ploegsteert Wood	10/12/1915	17/12/1915
War Diary	Le Gheer	18/10/1915	20/10/1915
War Diary	Ploegsteert Wood	21/12/1915	28/12/1915

1979/5

Brigade Machine Gun Coy (Coy Serj).

Aug 1916 – 1918 Feb

16TH DIVISION
49TH INFY BDE

49TH MACHINE GUN COY.
MAY 1916-FEB 1918

16TH DIVISION
49TH INFY BDE

Army Form C. 2118.

WAR DIARY
or
INTELLIGENCE SUMMARY
(Erase heading not required.)

49 Machine Gun Co. Vol 1

Instructions regarding War Diaries and Intelligence Summaries are contained in F.S. Regs., Part II. and the Staff Manual respectively. Title Pages will be prepared in manuscript.

Place	Date	Hour	Summary of Events and Information	Remarks and references to Appendices
Mazinghem Mazinghem	1st May 1916		"Rest" in billets. General fatigues on lorries and cleaning up. O.C. visited Trenches at Hulluch sector preparatory to taking over.	May 16
Mazinghem Munro	2nd May		"Rest" in billets. O.C. again visited trenches at Hulluch. Orders were received to relieve 48. M.G. Co.	
Mazinghem Munro	3rd May	8 a.m.	Parade for Trenches. Marched to Trenches and relieved 48. M.G. Co. Took over their positions	
Trenches Hulluch sector		9 p.m.	Relief finished.	
Trenches Hulluch sector	4 May		A fairly quiet day – except for slight artillery activity in the afternoon. Pte Woodgate shot an enemy sniper in the evening. Gas helmets were inspected by O.C. Sections.	

Army Form C. 2118.

WAR DIARY
or
INTELLIGENCE SUMMARY
(Erase heading not required.)

Instructions regarding War Diaries and Intelligence Summaries are contained in F. S. Regs, Part II. and the Staff Manual respectively. Title Pages will be prepared in manuscript.

Place	Date	Hour	Summary of Events and Information	Remarks and references to Appendices
Trenches Hulluch Sector	5 May 1916		Today was extremely quiet - only a few lydolite shells falling on and near the Hulluch road.	
	6 May	9 pm	47. M.G.C. started to relieve us	
		2 a.m	Relief finished - During this stay in the Trenches our casualties were NIL	
Noeux-les-Mines	6 May		Austin billets. The company arrived back in billets about 5. a.m. The company was not during the day.	
Noeux-les-Mines	7 May		The entire company worked on the Parade ground, horse lines and field kitchen. Backward men were instructed on the Guns.	
Noeux-les-Mines	8 May		General fatigue on horse lines and parade ground and field kitchen. Camp.	
Noeux-les-Mines	9 May		General fatigue on horse lines and a Company latrine.	

Army Form C. 2118.

WAR DIARY
or
INTELLIGENCE SUMMARY

(Erase heading not required.)

Instructions regarding War Diaries and Intelligence Summaries are contained in F. S. Regs., Part II. and the Staff Manual respectively. Title Pages will be prepared in manuscript.

Place	Date	Hour	Summary of Events and Information	Remarks and references to Appendices
Meaulte lez Mons	10 May 1916.	10 am	Company was inspected by G.O.C. 49th Bde.	
Meaulte lez Mons	11 May		General fatigues on Horse lines, field kitchens and Coy Latrines. Backward men continued their course on the Gun.	
Meaulte lez Mons	12 May	10 am	General work in Camp. Backward men fired a "course" on the Gun. Squad Drill formed for the company.	
		5 pm	Gas Helmet inspection.	
Meaulte lez Mons	13 May		General fatigues in Camp. Field kitchens completed.	
Meaulte lez Mons	14 May		General fatigues. Backward men continue on the Gun — Squad Drill.	

WAR DIARY
or
INTELLIGENCE SUMMARY

(Erase heading not required.)

Army Form C. 2118.

Place	Date	Hour	Summary of Events and Information	Remarks and references to Appendices
Mocurt-les-Mines	15 May 1916		General fatigues – Limbers were cleaned and oiled. "Backward" class carries on. O C Coy visits with O C 2 M.G. Coy, Loos sector M.G. emplacements etc, and positions to be taken up.	
Mocurt-les-Mines	16 May 1916		General fatigues on Horse Lines. "Backward" class continues. O C visits "village line" on Pt A7 and inspects positions to be taken up. O C also visits Commandant Bloos Defences and arranges for 2 guns to be under his command.	
Mocurt-les-Mines	17 May		Inspection of Kits, Gas Helmets and Webbt. Gunners thoroughly overhauled and tested. Limbers on parade. "C" Section took 2 Guns to Loos Defences to be under sole command of the Commandant. "D" Section took 2 Guns to relieve 2 Guns of A7 M.G. Coy.	

Army Form C. 2118.

WAR DIARY
or
INTELLIGENCE SUMMARY
(Erase heading not required.)

Instructions regarding War Diaries and Intelligence Summaries are contained in F.S. Regs., Part II and the Staff Manual respectively. Title Pages will be prepared in manuscript.

Place	Date	Hour	Summary of Events and Information	Remarks and references to Appendices
Noeux-les Mines Trenches Loos Sector.	18th May 1916.		Remainder of the Company relieves 2 M.G. Coy. w/18th the exception of 2 Guns and "B" Section who remain in reserve. This morning was spent getting guns in the Trenches.	
Trenches Loos.	19 May		Quiet day - Gun teams improved emplacements and dug-outs.	
Trenches Loos.	20 May		Quiet day. Gun alert from 8pm - 4 a.m. 21st. Reserve Trenches was shelled in the evening. Casualties Nil.	
Trenches Loos	21 May		Loos (again) received a slight shelling, but no M. Guns were hurt. 2 Guns fired 2250 rounds "indirect".	
Trenches Loos.	22 May	8 pm	There was slight artillery activity in the aftrnoon and evening round Maroc-in-gobelle with H.E and Tear Shells. Gas alarm and all emplacements were closed for Action - Casualties Nil.	

Army Form C. 2118.

WAR DIARY
or
INTELLIGENCE SUMMARY
(Erase heading not required.)

Instructions regarding War Diaries and Intelligence Summaries are contained in F. S. Regs., Part II. and the Staff Manual respectively. Title Pages will be prepared in manuscript.

Place	Date	Hour	Summary of Events and Information	Remarks and references to Appendices
Trenches Loos	23 May 1916		A fairly quiet day. M.G. 3 was transferred to M.G. 11 – new emplacement. R 8 and R 7 fired 750 rounds indirect.	
Trenches Loos	24 May		Quiet day. Good work carried on alternative emplacements. "Gearsmiths" wire machine. Threw out wire front line, wire. Dummy plain trenches were cheapener. 15 fresh o.r. joined for duty with 4 P.m.G. Coy.	
Trenches Loos	25 May		Quiet day. Trench towers were taken up and relaid. A covered emplacement was started on English alley. M.G. 8 fired 1500 rds indirect. M.G. 11 fired on a working party in the evening and observed some satisfactory result.	
Trenches Loos	26 May		A quiet day. Works continued as on M.G. 9, 10 – English alley. Infantry relief took place so there was no indirect fire. Q. new machines were drawn for the Q.M. helms to arms inspected by Sections.	
Trenches Loos	27 May		"B" Section took the 2 covered guns up to "Village Line". R 6 and M.G. 2 fired 1500 rounds indirect fire with good effect.	

Army Form C. 2118.

WAR DIARY
or
INTELLIGENCE SUMMARY
(Erase heading not required.)

Instructions regarding War Diaries and Intelligence Summaries are contained in F.S. Regs., Part II and the Staff Manual respectively. Title Pages will be prepared in manuscript.

Place	Date	Hour	Summary of Events and Information	Remarks and references to Appendices
Trenches Loos.	28 May 1916		Slight artillery activity on both sides. Two minenwerfer was fired in evening and another 2 Tanks.	
Trenches Loos.	29 May		Quiet day. Slight shelling in the Reserve Line near R.9. Goalpark was also on Dairy outs.	
Trenches Loos.	30 May		Quiet day. 4 gunsfire 2000 round fired closer R.10. Emplacement was found in. Except for overhead splinter proof – shelter –	

WAR DIARY
or
INTELLIGENCE SUMMARY
(Erase heading not required.)

49 Machine Gun Coy. Vol 2

Army Form C. 2118.

Place	Date	Hour	Summary of Events and Information	Remarks and references to Appendices
LOOS	1/6/16		Received orders to move Guns from Trenches to:- 12 Guns LOOS DEFENCES 4 Guns Village Line + Chalk Pit Alley, on night of 2/3rd. Inspected positions, issued necessary orders. Reports from Trenches indicate "General Quietude". Casualties NIL.	
"	2/6/16	11pm	Continued arrangements for relief. Guns in LOOS DEFENCES to be under sole control of Commandant LOOS. Relief being carried out satisfactorily.	
"	3/6/16	6am	Relief completed. Quiet day. 2nd Lieut Lane came out of Trenches with bad eyes. Another officer took his place. Casualties NIL.	
"	4/6/16		Inspected new positions. Good. Intermittent shelling - No firing from Guns.	
"	5/6/16		Everything reported quiet. Positions on VILLAGE LINE being improved. Some artillery during day.	
"	6/6/16		Quiet. Rearrangement of sections to enable men to be relieved occasionally. Guns in VILLAGE LINE & CHALK PIT ALLEY report Everything in order. Men working on emplacements & Dug outs.	R. W. Birch Cap

WAR DIARY or INTELLIGENCE SUMMARY

Army Form C. 2118.

49 Machine Gun Coy

Place	Date	Hour	Summary of Events and Information	Remarks and references to Appendices
Trenches LOOS	7/6/16	12	Guns in LOOS Defences under orders of Command out " " " Village Line & CHALK PIT ALLEY. Day very quiet.	
		11am	Telegram received announcing that reinforcement of 5 men would arrive at Bethune 1pm. Orders given for them to be met. Casualties NIL. 6 of 7 men sick in hospital 3 returned yesterday. 2nd Lieut Lane went to hospital today - Eyes.	
"	8/6/16		O.C. & 2nd inspected Gun positions in 14 Bis. Orders issued for relief. 2nd Lieut LANE evacuated.	
14 Bis	9/6/16		Relief completely 4pm. Immediately relief was completed 50 guns of Gun Trench opened heavy from Enemy artillery. No damage to our guns. One Gun fired during the night. Casualties NIL.	
"	10/6/16		A very quiet day - 50 rounds S.O.S. weather. Thunder lightning & very heavy rain. No gun fire - our infantry relief took place. O.C. inspected positions	
"	11/6/16		Nothing of any interest occurred. Rain - thunder &c. Casualties NIL.	

R. White
Capt

Army Form C. 2118.

WAR DIARY
or
INTELLIGENCE SUMMARY
(Erase heading not required.)

Ltg 11 G.G

Instructions regarding War Diaries and Intelligence Summaries are contained in F.S. Regs., Part II. and the Staff Manual respectively. Title Pages will be prepared in manuscript.

Place	Date	Hour	Summary of Events and Information	Remarks and references to Appendices
14 /31 S	12/6/16 13/6/16 14/6/16		Very bad weather — Everything quiet. work done on repairing Trenches &c. Casualties NIL	
	15/6/16		All Guns very active. R7 shot 2 Germans + dispersed many working parties. R2 dito. Helped artillery with barrage for a bombing raid which had to be abandoned however. Casualties NIL	
	16/6/16		Visited all Gun Positions. Everything alright. R2 fired a letter Observation Balloon — as wind was blowing him our way. The Germans pulled him in slightly — or took him back — any way he moved — R7 constantly firing at working parties. Cas. NIL.	
	17/6/16 18/6/16 19/6/16		Guns ordered not to fire these 3 days — after dusk things geophonally quiet — Guns fired very little in day time as no signs of a target. Cas: NIL.	
	20/6/16		Visited all Guns. all to fire again — indirect at Enemy comm. dumps to arranged targets. Cas NIL.	

R.W.Wapp

Army Form C. 2118.

WAR DIARY
or
INTELLIGENCE SUMMARY

(Erase heading not required.)

49 M.G.C.

Instructions regarding War Diaries and Intelligence Summaries are contained in F. S. Regs., Part II. and the Staff Manual respectively. Title Pages will be prepared in manuscript.

Place	Date	Hour	Summary of Events and Information	Remarks and references to Appendices
14 B I S.	21/6/16		Raids & gas attacks commenced. We continued to worry with our guns - getting a certain amount of retaliation which is always a fore sign, when the enemy has been successfully worried - He is distinctly suffering from nerves.	
	22/6/16			
	23/6/16		Guns still very active - Each gun now firing about 1-2000 rounds per night. Raids still continue. Casualties NIL.	
	24/6/16			
	25/6/16		We are relieved by H.S.Co. ½ our Coy comes out for rest - ½ to Loos defences under Command at LOOS. - for 8 days.	

R.L. Ault Cpl

WAR DIARY

49th Machine Gun Company

1st. July to 31st. July 1916.

VOLUME No. 3.

WAR DIARY
or
INTELLIGENCE SUMMARY
(Erase heading not required.)

Army Form C. 2118.

49 Machine Gun Co

Place	Date	Hour	Summary of Events and Information	Remarks and references to Appendices
Loos	1/7/16 2/7/16		Guns in Loos Defences under Cornwt	
"	3/7/16		Relieved 47 Coy Loos sector - all guns fired - impossible to see results - owing to our artillery activity	
"	4/7/16		Guns fired on enemys Comm" trenches - suspected dump - for the latter be retaliated for half an hour.	
"	5/7/16		Ditto - but we devoted more attention to our Right - with fairly good effect.	
"	6/7/16		Orders issued to fire on "lively spots" & keep it up in short bursts thro' the night. Had carefully noted & sent out a dozen places & ours having seen of these in period of from O.P.s in day time, to discover how much movement goes on.	
"	7/7/16			
"	8/7/16		All guns fires each night - we are gradually discovering enemys "sore spots".	
"	9/7/16 10/7/16		Continued firing by night on enemys Comm" trenches to keep his head down if possible.	

R.W.W.

Army Form C. 2118.

WAR DIARY
or
INTELLIGENCE SUMMARY
(Erase heading not required.)

49 Machine Gun Coy

Instructions regarding War Diaries and Intelligence Summaries are contained in F. S. Regs., Part II. and the Staff Manual respectively. Title Pages will be prepared in manuscript.

Place	Date	Hour	Summary of Events and Information	Remarks and references to Appendices
LOOS	11/7/16		Two quiet days & nights. We continue firing at night just to worry them.	
	12/7/16			
	13/7/16		Generally quiet all round. We fired all our guns at night as usual.	
	14/7/16		Guns did not fire as special arrangements had to be made for special operations for the next night. Two guns moved to front line in readiness.	
	15/7/16		We sprung a mine this morning & we in Coy made a raid. Two guns M.G. were sent up to front line to sweep enemy parapet - quite a success - we most certainly killed two of them. One of our aeroplanes fell on enemy front wire in flames.	
	17/7/16		Wet - Enemy very quiet - we did not fire our guns.	
	18/7/16		Relieved by 46 Coy. Guns did not fire - nothing to report.	
	19/7/16		The whole Coy goes to Noeux les Mines to rest. - (in reserve.)	

R. L. Pratt
Capt.

Army Form C. 2118.

WAR DIARY
or
INTELLIGENCE SUMMARY
(Erase heading not required.)

49 Machine Gun Coy.

Instructions regarding War Diaries and Intelligence Summaries are contained in F. S. Regs., Part II and the Staff Manual respectively. Title Pages will be prepared in manuscript.

Place	Date	Hour	Summary of Events and Information	Remarks and references to Appendices
Noeux	20/7/16		Resting – Baths – cleaning up	
Hulluch	21/7/16		We relieved 45 M.G. Co in Hulluch Sector. Guns fired at night at points given us by the relieved Coy.	
"	22/7/16		Our guns fired both by day & night – generally sweeping his trenches.	
"	23/7/16		We were relieved by 48 M.G.C. & proceeded to Noeux.	
Noeux	24/7/16 to 29/7/16		During these 6 days the whole time was spent in cleaning up, repairing &c – all men were thoroughly overhauled & cleaned – ditto guns limbers &c. Squads drilled daily & packing & unpacking limbers also.	
"	30/7/16		We relieved 47 M.G.C. in 14 BIS. Our Guns fired as usual.	
"	31/7/16		Knowing this particular area we continued to fire on points already proved as "Sore" – We continued this right thro' the night.	

R. Elliott Capt.
O.C. 49 M.G. Co.

Vol 4

WAR DIARY.

49th Machine Gun Company

MONTH OF AUGUST, 1916.

VOLUME :- 5

Army Form C. 2118.

WAR DIARY
or
INTELLIGENCE SUMMARY

(Erase heading not required.)

49 Machine Gun Coy

Place	Date	Hour	Summary of Events and Information	Remarks and references to Appendices
14 Bis	1/8/16 – 3/8/16		We continued to harass the enemy behind his lines, during these days. Retaliation was slight. Casualties nil.	
"	4/8/16 – 6/8/16		Front still very quiet. A great number of alternative machine gun emplacements were constructed, & from these points the enemy dumps & communications were harassed by day & by night. The enemy ineffectively tried to locate & destroy these positions. Work was general on the trenches & deep dug outs were constructed.	G.O Foulks Lt.

Army Form C. 2118.

WAR DIARY
or
INTELLIGENCE SUMMARY

(Erase heading not required.)

49 Machine Gun Coy.

Place	Date	Hour	Summary of Events and Information	Remarks and references to Appendices
14 Bus	7/8/16		A dummy raid was carried out in the night. Two of our guns assisted & fires from alternative emplacements in RESERVE TRENCH. The teams transfer their guns very well & fired 3,400 rounds in nine minutes. Only two very slight cross-feed stoppages occurred.	
"	8/8/16		The Headquarters of the Company moved from PHILOSOPHE EAST to PHILOSOPHE WEST. 1 Section & 1 gun in reserve at Headquarters.	
"	9/8/16		The guns fired at intervals during the night on the enemy's communications & dumps. The Section in reserve employes on improving their billets. 3 men to hospital — sick.	
"	10/8/16 11/8/16 12/8/16 13/8/16		During this period the whole front very quiet. Each night our guns continued to harass the enemy by firing on his communications & suspected dumps. 1 Officer to U.K - under age. 10 men to hospital - sick. G.O. Fairlie 2/Lt	

Army Form C. 2118.

WAR DIARY
or
INTELLIGENCE SUMMARY
(Erase heading not required.)

49 Machine Gun Coy.

Instructions regarding War Diaries and Intelligence Summaries are contained in F. S. Regs., Part II. and the Staff Manual respectively. Title Pages will be prepared in manuscript.

Place	Date	Hour	Summary of Events and Information	Remarks and references to Appendices
14 Bis	14/8/16		No change on our front, except a little increase in Air-craft activity —	
"	15/8/16 16/8/16 17/8/16 18/8/16		Orders were received, that, if wind + weather was favourable, gas would be used on the enemy. M.G. Coys were to fire sufficiently to drown the noise of discharge. Both wind + weather were unfavourable. — Usual harassing fire 3 men discharged from hospital.	
"	19/8/16		Front still quiet — Repairs in trenches.	
"	20/8/16		Gas went over + the raiding party was sent over. Results uncertain. 1 man accidentally wounded.	
"	21/8/16 22/8/16		No change in our front. 7 Reinforcements arrived from England.	
"	23/8/16		Still no change. Orders received that a relief would take place the next day. Go Faiths 24.	

WAR DIARY
or
INTELLIGENCE SUMMARY

(Erase heading not required.)

Army Form C. 2118.

49 Machine Gun Coy.

Place	Date	Hour	Summary of Events and Information	Remarks and references to Appendices
Noeux-les-Mines	24/8/16		Relief completed by 3 p.m. + the Company moved into NOEUX-LES-MINES. Relieving Company - 112 M.G. Coy.	
"	25/8/16		The entire day was spent on packing etc, ready for our move on the following day.	
"	26/8/16		The Company paraded at 3 p.m. + marches out of NOEUX-LES-MINES at 3.15 p.m. It arrived at MARLES-LES-MINES at 6-30 p.m. At 9 a.m a billetting party left NOEUX + met us upon our arrival at MARLES. The whole company was comfortably in billets by 7 p.m. The billets were spacious + very clean.	
Marles-les-Mines	27/8/16		The Company rested. It bathed at 2.30 p.m + was payed-out. 1 man admitted to hospital.	
"	28/8/16		Orders were received that the company would leave MARLES-LES-MINES. It paraded at 6.30 p.m + marches to FOUQUEREUIL, arriving there at 9 p.m. G.O Faulu Lt.	

Army Form C. 2118.

WAR DIARY
or
INTELLIGENCE SUMMARY
(Erase heading not required.)

49 Machine Gun Coy

Place	Date	Hour	Summary of Events and Information	Remarks and references to Appendices
—	29/8/16		The Company entrained at FOUQUEREUIL at 12.15"a.m. & detrained at LONGNEAU at 8.30 a.m. From there it marched to SAILLY-LE-SEC arriving at 7.30 p.m. The village was small, but comfortable billets were eventually found for the men.	
Sailly-le-Sec	30/8/16		The Company rested. There was a foot inspection in the afternoon.	
—	31/8/16		Orders were received to move. The Company paraded at 8.15"a.m. & marched to the Camping Grounds at the HAPPY VALLEY. It arrived there at 12 noon. The afternoon was spent in improving the Camp.	

R. W. Scott Capt
O.C. 49 M.G.C.

WAR DIARY

H.Q. Machine Gun Company

FOR MONTH OF SEPTEMBER, 1916.

VOLUME

Army Form C. 2118.

WAR DIARY
or
INTELLIGENCE SUMMARY

(Erase heading not required.)

Instructions regarding War Diaries and Intelligence Summaries are contained in F. S. Regs., Part II. and the Staff Manual respectively. Title Pages will be prepared in manuscript.

Place	Date	Hour	Summary of Events and Information	Remarks and references to Appendices
Rest at Gibraltar	1/9/16		Restry Parades 9 a.m inspection of accoutrements & feet 2 p.m Gun Drill etc	
Rest at Gibraltar	2/9/16		Restry Parades Drill etc	
	3/9/16		Moved to Citadel & left at night to Billon Farm	
Billon Farm	4/9/16		Left in the afternoon received orders to proceed to Guillemont. Journey wet. Journey took 12 hours	
In the field	5/9/16		Guillemont Pte J Phillips missing " Cross Thrill Shoot " W Scott Wounded Shrapnel	
In the field	6/9/16		Guillemont Coy Sgt Major Muller wounded Shrapnel Sgt Effron "	

WAR DIARY
or
INTELLIGENCE SUMMARY
(Erase heading not required.)

Army Form C. 2118.

Place	Date	Hour	Summary of Events and Information	Remarks and references to Appendices
In the Field	4/9/16		Relieved from Guillemont line by 2/ 166th and 147th Bdys & moved to Billon Farm. Killed 2/Lt Boardham " Hodges " Williams Sgt Hodgets Wounded J. Hill	
Resting at Billon Farm	5/9/16		Resting in Billon Farm 2/16 Barley killed by shell cleaning up. Returned to Guillemont & Trones Wood. 8pm 2 guns reported to each Batln (4 Battns in line) remainder in reserve at Tronces Trench under 2 guns to 17th Royal Irish Fusiliers 2 " " 1 " Royal Inniskillings 2 " " 8 " Royal Irish Fusiliers 2 " " 6 Royal Inniskillings	

Army Form C. 2118.

WAR DIARY
or
INTELLIGENCE SUMMARY
(Erase heading not required.)

3

Instructions regarding War Diaries and Intelligence Summaries are contained in F.S. Regs., Part II. and the Staff Manual respectively. Title Pages will be prepared in manuscript.

Place	Date	Hour	Summary of Events and Information	Remarks and references to Appendices
In the field	9/9/16		Relief complete and all guns in position by 1 am at full & exclusive report on this days work will follow	
do	10/9/16		Teams all returned with guns during the early morning except 6.T. which arrived at 2pm. Roll-call at 3pm. Casualties as follows: Sgt Powell wounded Pte McKenzie " " Calum " " Wavell " " Fletcher " " Price " " Ruthven " & missing afterwards found in S.B.S. Pte Yates missing Corpl Jackson killed March Pte Murphy do	

Army Form C. 2118.

WAR DIARY
or
INTELLIGENCE SUMMARY
(Erase heading not required.)

4

Instructions regarding War Diaries and Intelligence Summaries are contained in F. S. Regs., Part II. and the Staff Manual respectively. Title Pages will be prepared in manuscript.

Place	Date	Hour	Summary of Events and Information	Remarks and references to Appendices
Sailly Le Sec	11/9/16		Left Billon Farm 4.30 for Sailly Le Sec arriving at 10 pm	
	12/9/16		Resting & cleaning up. Reinforcements 2 Officers 2/Lt A.G King and 32 men attached	to Division
Sailly Le Sec	13/9/16		Cleaning guns, Limbers, wackery & Gun Drill	
do	14/9/16		Cleaning Equipment Reinforcements 2 Officers 2/Lt W Robinson & 2/Lt E.H. Simpson	
do	15/9/16		Company at 9.30 am for C.O.'s inspection. Reinforcement of 66 men arrived	
do	16/9/16		Company paraded for Baths at 9.30 am & marched to Corbie returning at 2.30 pm.	

Army Form C. 2118.

WAR DIARY
or
INTELLIGENCE SUMMARY
(Erase heading not required.)

Place	Date	Hour	Summary of Events and Information	Remarks and references to Appendices
Laity de Sec	17/9/16		Transport paraded at 1.30 pm to proceed to Wanel	
do	18/9/16		Company paraded at 9.45 am to march to lorries arrived at lorries at 1.10 pm, took lorries at lorries at 2.30 pm for Wanel arrived at Wanel at 6.30 pm fellows for two nights very wet weather. Transport arrived at Wanel at 7.30 pm	
Wanel	19/9/16		Company resting & general cleaning up	Reinforcements 14 men arrived
Wanel	20/9/16		Company paraded at 9am to clean equipment 2pm for equipment inspection Gas Helmet, Iron Rations, ammunition, Rifle & Revolver inspection by section Commanders	Reinforcements 2 Officers 2 Lt S J Hoare 2 Lt D B Bellamy

Army Form C. 2118.

WAR DIARY
or
INTELLIGENCE SUMMARY

(Erase heading not required.)

Instructions regarding War Diaries and Intelligence Summaries are contained in F. S. Regs., Part II. and the Staff Manual respectively. Title Pages will be prepared in manuscript.

Place	Date	Hour	Summary of Events and Information	Remarks and references to Appendices
Warul	21/9/16		Company paraded at 2am to march to Pont Remy Station entrained for Bailleul at 6.25 am, arrived Bailleul at 4.15 pm detrained & marched to billets	
Renmel	22/9/16		Company paraded at 8.30 am for trenches and relieved the 12th Canadian at B. Coy	
do	23/9/16		14 guns in the trenches. 2 in reserve at Bay Headquarters	
do	24/9/16		14 guns in the line 2 in reserve during the night 23/24th we fired on cross Roads strong points & searched enemy trenches.	
do	25/9/16		14 guns in the line & 2 in reserve we continued to fire on cross roads & searching enemy trenches	

2449 Wt. W14957/M90 750,000 1/16 J.B.C. & A. Forms/C.2118/12.

WAR DIARY or INTELLIGENCE SUMMARY

Army Form C. 2118.

(Erase heading not required.)

Place	Date	Hour	Summary of Events and Information	Remarks and references to Appendices
Hamel	26/9/16		14 Bns in the line & 2 in reserve during the night we continued to harry the enemy by fire on roads & railways (light), & communication trenches. One gun exploded & another being so damaged that only one gun remains	
do	27/9/16		14 Bns in the line 2 in reserve. Night fairly quiet. Trenches & dumps	
do	28/9/16		A 8" shell burst within five of our guns. Two to be sent away to new emplacements at ____ 6 guns in the line + 1 in reserve at HQ. Night otherwise quiet. Enemy roads	
do	29/9/16		6 guns in the line. You reserve during the night 28/29 our fire on enemy roads, railways, dumps & bone points. Teams in enemy lines keeping up a good rate of fire.	

Army Form C. 2118.

WAR DIARY
or
INTELLIGENCE SUMMARY
(Erase heading not required.)

Place	Date	Hour	Summary of Events and Information	Remarks and references to Appendices
Kemmel	3/9/16		Inter company relief. Relief completed.	
			10 guns in the line 16 in reserve at Coy H.Q during the night	
		29/30	our snipers the enemy by fires on his front lines	
			Also on roads & open. Much during no + spare fire	

M. Maurippe Capt.
O.C. 49 M.G. Co.

49th MACHINE GUN COMPANY.

REPORT ON OPERATIONS 8th to 10th SEPTEMBER 1916.

PRELIMINARY DISPOSITIONS.

Two guns under 2/Lt. FAIRLIE G.O. detailed to the 7th R.IRISH.FUS.

Two guns under 2/Lt. BREWSTER H.P. detailed to the 8th INNISKILLINGS

Two guns under 2/Lt. SADDLETON W.H. detailed to the 7th INNISKILLING

Two guns under 2/Lt. MORRISON T. detailed to the 8th R.IRISH FUS.

Eight guns under 2/Lt. BRACEWELL A. detailed to act as Brigade Res.

All details were in position before 5 a.m. 9th September.

2/Lt. FAIRLIE at QUARRIES T.19.c.2.3.

2/Lt. BREWSTER in trenches to the north of Quarries.

2/Lt. SADDLETON in CEMETERY T.19.d.7.3.

2/Lt. MORRISON in ARROW HEAD COPSE.

2/LT. BRACEWELL in Sherwood Trench, near GUILLEMONT ROAD.

Machine Gun H.Q. was also in SHERWOOD TRENCH.

DETAIL OF ACTION taken by various sub-sections.

2/Lt. FAIRLIE.   Advanced with 7th R. I. F. about 4.30.p.m.
9th September to Support position T.19.a.7.7. at 4.30.p.m. pushed
forward through enemy artillery barrage into GINCHY, taking up
second line position along road T.13.d.2.8. to T.13.d.7.4. during
this last advance lost touch with 7th R. I. F. but when in position
along road reported to O.C. Royal Irish Rifles, and kept guns in
readiness during fluctuations of engagement to repel any counter-
attack.   Relieved by WELSH GUARDS about 1 a.m. 10th September,
their Vickers guns taking over positions vacated.

2/Lt. BREWSTER.   Remained in position in and about the QUARRIES
until 4.30 p.m. 9th September 1916.
Whilst in this position one gun team was buried, they were got
out and replaced from reserve.
Advanced at 4.30 p.m with 8th INNISKILLINGS into position to right
of GINCHY, here dug themselves in and consolidated positions to
withstand counter-attack.   During the advance one gun team was
separated and buried by a shell, they were got out and fell back
into Brigade reserve (see latter)   (sniper,
When in position to right of GINCHY 2/LT. BREWSTER was killed by
whilst searching for missing gun team in rear of his position.
This gun team was thus left in charge of SGT.VICK who organized
search party through village for snipers, kept gun team together
and brought gun and team out safely when the INNISKILLINGS were
relieved.

2/Lt. SADDLETON.   Remained in position in CEMETERY until about
4.30 p.m. 9th September, then moved with the 7th INNISKILLINGS into
position in front and to the right of GINCHY with one gun, with
this gun searching fire was applied, about 30 belts being fired.

- 2 -

  Whilst in this position Lt. SADDLETON bound up the wounds of any men falling back, this being done under heavy shell fire.
  Whilst making arrangements for his rear guns advance, 2/Ltd. SADDLETON was slightly wounded. Cpl. SLOCOMBE was then left in charge of one gun and Pte. Thrale of the other. These men safely brought out guns and teams about 6 a.m. 10 Sept.

LT. MORRISON. Remained in position in ARROW HEAD COPSE until about 7 p.m. 9th Sept. whilst here one team was buried by shell, they were got out, but two men were badly wounded.
  At 7 p.m. advanced with 8th R.I.Fus. through heavily shelled area into position near SUNK ROAD in front of LONE TREE, here the guns were kept in readiness to be pushed forward to any threatened positions.
  After the R.I,Fs. were relieved LT. MORRISON brought out his guns and teams.

2/Lt. BRACEWELL. During 9th September reinforcements were sent to 2/Lt. BREWSTER to replace buried team. The team belonging to 2/Lt. BREWSTER which was buried and fell back onto reserve, was reorganized and reinforced and sent back to battle position and fired as targets presented themselves until all ammunition was exhausted, then safely brought out gun team.
  Ammunition parties were organized and despatched to various guns during the day, men from the company transport being particularly useful in this respect, these parties often proceeded under heavy shell fire.
  When relief was ordered, limbers were brought up close to TRONES WOOD and the GUILLEMONT Rd. patrolled.

  O.C. Company personally conducted the company on the night of 8th September, established H.Q. in SHERWOOD trench and kept in touch with during operations with the various section officers.

         (Sd) R.
            Capt.
      O.C. 49 M.G.C oy.

Army Form C. 2118.

16 / Vol 6

WAR DIARY
or
INTELLIGENCE SUMMARY

(Erase heading not required.) of 49th Machine Gun Coy for October 1916

Instructions regarding War Diaries and Intelligence Summaries are contained in F. S. Regs., Part II. and the Staff Manual respectively. Title Pages will be prepared in manuscript.

Place	Date	Hour	Summary of Events and Information	Remarks and references to Appendices
Kemmel	1/10/16		10 Guns in the line – 6 in reserve at Bay H.Q.	
do	2/10/16		During the night we fired on Enemy Tracks + Cross Roads	
do	3/10/16		During the night we continued to fire on Enemy's Working parties, Tracks + Roadways. Searching Communication Trenches + firing on Cross Roads.	
do	4/10/16		We did not fire during the night but kept all guns in readiness	
do	5/10/16		During the night we fired on Enemy Inspection Parties Dumps, on night Working, Searched his Communication Trenches, + also fired on Cross Roads	
do	6/10/16		Firing during the night on Cross Roads, Searched Road leading to WYTSCHAETE also on Junction of Roads. M. Glass on the Trazel. 10 Guns in the line + 6 in reserve at Coy H.Q. During the night we Vertically searched Enemys Communication Trenches, + searched along his roads.	
do	7/10/16		During the night we fired on Lamp Signs + gave Enemy fire is a patrol of the 8 th Dublin Fusiliers Company.	

R.V. Dell
Lieut O.C.
O.C. 49 M.G. Co.

Army Form C. 2118.

WAR DIARY
or
INTELLIGENCE SUMMARY
(Erase heading not required.)

Place	Date	Hour	Summary of Events and Information	Remarks and references to Appendices
Kemmel	8/10/16		During the night our gun at N.23 d. 1.3. fired at, and silenced an enemy machine gun they from N 30 a. 4. 3. This enemy gun had been causing considerable damage round about N.23.c.8.5. The enemy having registered our emplacement the previous night & made 1 direct hit with his heavy artillery. We also fired on suspected enemy sniper post, on suspected machine gun emplacements in PECHHAM; exploded roads & gave covering fire to patrols.	
do	9/10/16		During the night we exploded enemy cross roads, opened occasional bursts of m.g. to impede the occasionally happening to enemy working parties and also ranged on enemy emplacement for emergency fire. We also ranged on enemy known from time sniping places.	
do	10/10/16		We continued to search & traverse known roads; opened burst of m.g. on MADELSTEAD FARM.	
do	11/10/16		During the night we fired on PETIT BOIS, on cross roads leading to WYTCHAETE traversed enemy roads & fired on enemy tracks	

R. L. Bell
Major
O.C. 49 M.G. Co.

Army Form C. 2118.

WAR DIARY
or
INTELLIGENCE SUMMARY

(Erase heading not required.)

Instructions regarding War Diaries and Intelligence Summaries are contained in F. S. Regs., Part II. and the Staff Manual respectively. Title Pages will be prepared in manuscript.

Place	Date	Hour	Summary of Events and Information	Remarks and references to Appendices
Kemmel	12/10/16		All teams on the trenches received 1/3 teams on the toes + 6 in reserve at Coy HQ. During the night we continued to worry the enemy by traversing and searching roads + firing on cross roads	
do	13/10/16		Night firing on Grange Road + Grove Road adjacent to WYTSCHAETE + on targets in O.14.d.	
do	14/10/16		We again were busy during the "night" on his roads + during the night we searched + traversed them especially Grange and WYTSCHAETE	
do	15/10/16		Orders that Hostile fire was supposed or couraged + co-operated by firing by Regt on fixed Rgt. Target + copies received + adopted advising us to open up on WHITE HOUSE + copses charges + opened up as before.	
do	16/10/16		During the night we were by means of careful traverses on roads of fired upon before	
do	17/10/16			
do	18/10/16		During Dawn alert joint Bombardment on front on enemy communication trenches, strong points switches was replied to by supports + ? machine guns ? crossings	

R. Hill Major
O.C. 49 M.G. Co.

Army Form C. 2118.

WAR DIARY
or
INTELLIGENCE SUMMARY

(Erase heading not required.)

Place	Date	Hour	Summary of Events and Information	Remarks and references to Appendices
Kemmel	18/10/16		+ during the night we tracks well by the enemy	
do	19/10/16		Night firing on Roads in WYTSCHAETE + Paces in Bois Woods	
do	20/10/16		We fired on Enemy Working Parties during the night Transverse roads	
do	21/10/16		We continue to reply the enemy by firing on lorries at BONE POINT searched Wood + Railway + enemy Paces opened at OHIO POINT	
do	22/10/16		During the night we fired on OHIO POINT	
do	23/10/16		We harassed Roads used by the enemy + also on HAG POINT	
do	24/10/16		During the night we fired on JUMP POINT + searched Woods + Railway at O.19.c.o.4. all teams on the line relieved 10 guns on the line + 6 in reserve at coy. H.Q.	
do	25/10/16		We fired on Roads + Railways during the night	
do	26/10/16		Night firing on enemy Cross Roads + into WYTSCHAETE	

L.A. Quill Major
O.C. 49 M.G. Co.

Army Form C. 2118.

WAR DIARY
or
INTELLIGENCE SUMMARY
(Erase heading not required.)

#49 M.G.C.   Oct 1916

Place	Date	Hour	Summary of Events and Information	Remarks and references to Appendices
Hamel	27 / 28		Our own firing took place each night on Enemy's comm? trenches - dumps - roads &c	
"	29		During day portions were reconnoitred and from battle portions and later a certain percentage of guns were laid to search possible lines of approach and main communication trenches and supports. The remainder were laid to search enemy front parapet and NO MANS LAND. They were also so arranged as to be able to bring fire to bear on ground that would have to be crossed by any counter-attack. All guns opened rapid fire at 5·45 p.m. on points allocated to. three minutes, and then continued with systematic bursts until raid was over; also during remainder of night bursts of fire were applied at irregular intervals.	
"	30		Quiet day - Guns did not fire - Relief took place.	
"	31		During the night Guns fired in support of L & R Brigades raids	R de Pratt [?] —Maj or O.C. 49 M.G. Co.

WAR DIARY
or
INTELLIGENCE SUMMARY

Army Form C. 2118.

4 M G Coy

(Erase heading not required.)

of the 49th Machine Gun Coy. November 1916

Place	Date	Hour	Summary of Events and Information	Remarks and references to Appendices
Nsomel	1/11/16		10 Guns in the line, 6 in reserve at Company Headquarters. During the night we fired on Enemys Gun Posts & reported no news.	
	2/11/16		Night firing on tracks used by the Enemy & on roads	
	3/11/16		We fired on Enemys Gun Posts and communication trenches	
	4/11/16		During the night we fired on Enemy Gun Posts. Relief commenced between trenches & on Railway. Duke of Connaught visited the line.	
	5/11/16		3rd Coy Company relief all guns between & trenches. 10 guns in the line & 6 in reserve at Coy HQ	
	6/11/16		During the night we manned the Enemy high flying on the cross roads and tracks	
	7/11/16		Night firing on enemys communication trenches	
	8/11/16		During the night we fired on Enemys Stray Posts and cross roads	

Army Form C. 2118.

WAR DIARY
or
INTELLIGENCE SUMMARY

(Erase heading not required.)

Instructions regarding War Diaries and Intelligence Summaries are contained in F. S. Regs., Part II. and the Staff Manual respectively. Title Pages will be prepared in manuscript.

Place	Date	Hour	Summary of Events and Information	Remarks and references to Appendices
Kemmel	9/1/16		We fired on SCOTFARM and trenches adjacent to SKIP POINT during the night	
	10/1/16		During the night we fired on Enemys Roads and Tracks also on RAG POINT and BONE POINT	
	11/1/16		Inter company relief all gun teams relieved 10 teams in the trenches at Company HQ. During the night we fired on Enemys Headquarters, Ammunition Trenches, Cross Roads & Tracks Points	
	12/1/16		Night firing on JUMP POINT and adjacent trenches	
	13/1/16		We fired on Enemys trenches adjoining JUMP POINT also on dump at BONE POINT during the night	
	14/1/16		Night firing on Enemys Cross Roads	
	15/1/16		During the night we traversed Enemys Roads	
	16/1/16		Firing during Starshead on Dock House & on Enemys Cross Roads	

Army Form C. 2118.

WAR DIARY
or
INTELLIGENCE SUMMARY (3)
(Erase heading not required.)

Place	Date	Hour	Summary of Events and Information	Remarks and references to Appendices
Tunnel	17/11/16		Sub Company Relief 10 guns on the line 6 in reserve at Coy H.Q. Firing on Enemys Trench Tramway & between two stone bridges.	
	18/11/16		Night firing on Enemys Trench Railway System.	
	19/11/16		During the night we fired on Enemys Trench Railway Tramway & were attention to Crossings.	
	20/11/16		We fired on Enemys Tramway Crossing & Cross Roads.	
	21/11/16		Barrage fire Registration commenced, night firing on Enemys Trench Railways & on a Light which appeared near HOSPICE	
	22/11/16		We had a Special ashoot on the Enemys Trench Tramways & took all Guns up to the line for this Into Company Relief	
	23/11/16		10 Guns on the line 6 in reserve at Coy H.Q. Enemy Gunnery Raid we co-operated by firing on Enemys Trench Railway System	

Army Form C. 2118.

WAR DIARY
or
INTELLIGENCE SUMMARY

(Erase heading not required.)

Instructions regarding War Diaries and Intelligence Summaries are contained in F. S. Regs., Part II. and the Staff Manual respectively. Title Pages will be prepared in manuscript.

Place	Date	Hour	Summary of Events and Information	Remarks and references to Appendices
Kimmio	24/11/16		We again fired on Enemy's French Railways.	
	25/11/16		During the night we fired on Enemy's French Railways, searching Roads & also on Cross Roads.	
	26/11/16		We fired on Enemy's Roads & Railways during the night.	
	27/11/16		We traversed Enemy Reserve trenches & fired on his Lorry point.	
	28/11/16		Fired on White House, being used by the enemy, & searched the roads.	
	29/11/16		During the night we fired on Enemy's Cross Roads, Railway & Roads.	
	30/11/16		3rew Company Relief. 10 turns in the line 6 in reserve at Bay 14. Night firing on Roads & French Railways.	

WAR DIARY FOR MONTH OF DECEMBER, 1916.

VOLUME 9

HQ Machine Gun Company

Army Form C. 2118.

WAR DIARY
or
INTELLIGENCE SUMMARY

(Erase heading not required.)

Of the 49th Machine Gun Coy For December 1916

Instructions regarding War Diaries and Intelligence Summaries are contained in F. S. Regs., Part II. and the Staff Manual respectively. Title Pages will be prepared in manuscript.

Place	Date	Hour	Summary of Events and Information	Remarks and references to Appendices
KEMMEL	1/12/16	10 am	On the line & in reserve at Bgd Headquarters. Nipper firing on Enemy Railway Tramways & Junctions & on his earthworks.	
	2/12/16		During the night we fired on the enemy tramway Railways & Roads	
	3/12/16		We fired on paths & tracks and on roads & Railways in the enemy lines	
	4/12/16		Night firing on the Enemy front line between PECKHAM and SPANBROEK - MOLEN also on two railways & tramways & track works	
	5/12/16		Reorganization of front & telling of positions formerly held by the 4.5th M.G. Coy. During the night we fired on Enemy cross Roads, Railways, Tramways & Roads & earthworks.	
	6/12/16		Smith Company relief all Gun Teams Relieved. Night firing on Enemy Enemy M.G. emplacement, Roads, Tramways Roads dealing with WYTSCHAETE	

Army Form C. 2118.

WAR DIARY
or
INTELLIGENCE SUMMARY

(Erase heading not required.)

of the 10th Howitzer Battery

Instructions regarding War Diaries and Intelligence Summaries are contained in F. S. Regs., Part II. and the Staff Manual respectively. Title Pages will be prepared in manuscript.

Place	Date	Hour	Summary of Events and Information	Remarks and references to Appendices
NEWALA	7/12/16		We again fired on Enemy's Railways, Braw Roads, & on WHITE HOUSE	
	8/12/16		Firing on Enemy Roads, Trenches & Railways during the night	
	9/12/16		Re arrangement of guns under new system. 8 guns in Battle Position. 6 in reserve positions, 2 in reserve at Bry H.Q. We again fired on Enemy's Roads, Cross Roads & Railways	
	10/12/16		Night firing on Enemy's Trench Railways	
	11/12/16		Our Teams & Reserve Positions returned, after 48 hours in those positions. We fired on Roads & Trench Railways during the night	
	12/12/16		Gun-supporting Relief. 8 guns in Battle Position at Bry H.Q. Hearing Enemy hurrying on bearers, we fired on their hurried conveyances by our usual effort [illegible] Enemy niece no [illegible]	

WAR DIARY or INTELLIGENCE SUMMARY

Army Form C. 2118.

(Erase heading not required.)

of the 4th + Wiltshire Regt. Regt.

Place	Date	Hour	Summary of Events and Information	Remarks and references to Appendices
KEMMEL	13/2/16		Firing on Enemys Firing Posts during the day.	
	14/2/16		During the night we again fired on Enemys Firing Posts Railways.	
	15/2/16		Firing on Roads & Enemy Front Railways	
	16/2/16		We fired on Enemys Railways & Firing points during the night	
	17/2/16		Firing on Enemys Railways approx three batteries L'ENFER WOOD area near 13,000	
	18/2/16		During the night we fired on Enemys Earthworks, Paths & tracks near by him	
	19/2/16		We fired on Enemys roads, Railways & trenches.	
	20/2/16		'A' Coy Capt Phillip & guns in Battle positions & in reserve positions two in reserve at Bty. H.Q. We fired on WYTSCHAETE CROSS ROADS & other Roads seen by them	

Army Form C. 2118.

WAR DIARY
or
INTELLIGENCE SUMMARY

(Erase heading not required.)

of the 16th Machine Gun Coy

Instructions regarding War Diaries and Intelligence Summaries are contained in F. S. Regs., Part II. and the Staff Manual respectively. Title Pages will be prepared in manuscript.

Place	Date	Hour	Summary of Events and Information	Remarks and references to Appendices
KEMMEL	21/12/16		Night firing on Enemy Trench Railways & Reserve Roads	
	22/12/16		Fired on Enemy Trench Railways	
	23/12/16		During the night we fired on roads used by the Enemy	
	24/12/16		We again fired on Enemy Railways	
	25/12/16		During darkness we fired on an Enemy Tramway in construction & on an Wendra rear	
	26/12/16		We fired on suspected Tramway & on track running along the edge of Bois du WYTSCHAETE along which Enemy were seen walking; also on Farm where troops were observed dashing about 40yds apparently from one trench to another	
	27/12/16		Enter temporary Relief 8 Guns in Battle Positions. 6 in Reserve positions & 2 in reserve at Bay H.Q. Firing on Enemy Trench Railways.	

2449 Wt. W14957/M90 750,000 1/16 J.B.C. & A. Forms/C.2118/12.

Army Form C. 2118.

WAR DIARY
or
INTELLIGENCE SUMMARY
(Erase heading not required.)

Instructions regarding War Diaries and Intelligence Summaries are contained in F.S. Regs., Part II. and the Staff Manual respectively. Title Pages will be prepared in manuscript.

5/ of The 49th Machine Gun Coy

Place	Date	Hour	Summary of Events and Information	Remarks and references to Appendices
KEMMEL	25/12/16		Night firing on Enemy's trench Railways & Roads	
	26/12/16		During trench Mortar + Artillery Bombardments we co-operated by harassing Enemy's Front & Support lines = on his support trenches between PECKHAM and SPANBROEKMOLEN	
			On the 9pm Bombardment	
			We again traversed his Front & Support lines & also fired on Known areas by him	
			During the Night all fires on tracks behind PETIT PUIS, + LENFER WOOD made about COX FARM & his tramways runs about SCOTT FARM	
	30/12/16		Firing on Enemy points Railways & Cross Roads	
	31/12/16		We again fire on Enemy trench Railways + on WYTSCHAETE tramways	

O.C. 49 M.G. Coy

WAR DIARY for month of JANUARY, 1917.

VOLUME 10

49th Machine Gun Company

Army Form C. 2118.

WAR DIARY
or
INTELLIGENCE SUMMARY by 49 Corps. M.G.C. (Cont)

(Erase heading not required.)

Instructions regarding War Diaries and Intelligence Summaries are contained in F.S. Regs., Part II. and the Staff Manual respectively. Title Pages will be prepared in manuscript.

Place	Date	Hour	Summary of Events and Information	Remarks and references to Appendices
WYTSCHAETE SECTOR	1/1/17 to 11/1/17		Applied indirect fire each night onto Roads Trench Railways. Support and Reserve lines and communication trenches. Headquarters, Dumps in Enemy lines. Map Squares O.19: O.13: O.25: O.26: O.20: N.30: N.24.	
do.	12/1/17		Applied overhead support, flanking and covering fire for our reconnoitring parties. 30,000 rds. being fired in and about SPANBROEKMOLEN N 30 a and b and MAEDELSTEDE N 24 c and d.	
do	13/1/17 16/1/17		Applied indirect fire each night and during daylight onto working parties, roads trench railways, sidings, strong points in Enemy lines. Map squares as detailed above.	
do	17/1/17	4.30 9.0	Carried out during night 17/18 a scheme of fire, applied to Return Dumps and Roads and railways leading thereto with respect to these being formed from reports of encampments of prisoners.	
do	19/1/17 to 23/1/17		Applied overhead fire each night and during daylight onto Commands, trench railways Screened roads. Dumps, Paths, Strong points in enemy lines. also frequently applied barrage fire on enemy front line and NO MANS LAND. Frequently drove off enemy aeroplanes with M.G. fire.	
do	24/1/17	11.35AM	Action taken during test attack training two reserve positions taken up, guns in the line armed and all necessary action taken in 30 mins.	
do	25/1/17	6.30pm	Applied overhead fire in conjunction with the Artillery onto suspected enemy treks. Various relief on all roads in N 36 b. N30d. O.31 c. O.19 c &d. O 28 a. O.25 c.	
do	26/1/17		Applied indirect fire into Strong Points and trenches in O.25 a. N 30 d.	
do	27/1/17		Applied overhead fire in conjunction with our artillery onto suspected enemy field kitchens in O.19 d. 15.90	

A Blackwell Lt.
49 M.G.C.

Army Form C. 2118.

WAR DIARY
or
INTELLIGENCE SUMMARY by 49 Coy. M.G.C. (cont)

(Erase heading not required.)

Instructions regarding War Diaries and Intelligence Summaries are contained in F. S. Regs., Part II. and the Staff Manual respectively. Title Pages will be prepared in manuscript.

Place	Date	Hour	Summary of Events and Information	Remarks and references to Appendices
WYTSCHAETE SECTOR	29/1/17	11 AM	Front line barrage fire tried, good observation being obtained on the snow. Applied overhead fire during night onto roads in O.19.d.	
do.	29/1/17 to 31/1/17		Applied indirect overhead fire onto roads and transport in O.25.a. to O.19.d.	

R. McArthur Major
O.C. 49 M.G. Coy

WAR DIARY.

FOR MONTH OF FEBRUARY, 1917.

VOLUME 11

UNIT:- 149th Machine Gun Company

Army Form C. 2118.

WAR DIARY
or
INTELLIGENCE SUMMARY
(Erase heading not required.)

49 Coy. M.G.C.

Instructions regarding War Diaries and Intelligence Summaries are contained in F.S. Regs., Part II. and the Staff Manual respectively. Title Pages will be prepared in manuscript.

Place	Date	Hour	Summary of Events and Information	Remarks and references to Appendices
WYTSCHAETE SECTOR	Feb 1st 1917	5.20AM	Attempted raid by the enemy; after preliminary bombardment. S.O.S. signal was sent up by our own infantry on the front line and instantly our first system of machine guns opened barrage fire on enemy front line area. NO MANS LAND along the whole brigade front, our support and reserve system of guns took up the firing and by 5.30 AM (ends. the front line barrage opened at 5.20 AM) the enemy support, reserve and all tracks, railways & roads were being swept with fire. 17,000 rounds were fired during the engagement. The enemy did not succeed in entering our trenches & left many dead in No Mans Land.	
Do	2/2/17 to 3/2/17		Guns fired during day and night at intervals onto dumps, tramways, crossroads & roads	
Do	4/2/17 to 6/2/17		A scheme of fire was carried out onto enemy dumps. Roads & crossroads, & suspected wiring parties. On the 6th L'ENFER WOOD was fired onto. Observation from Artillery O.P. on KEMMEL HILL being obtained.	
Do	7/2/17 to 10/2/17		Guns fired during day & night at intervals onto dumps, tramways, crossroads & roads.	
Do	11/2/17 to 13/2/17		An enemy relief being expected on this night, all roads leading to the sector were fired onto at intervals during darkness.	
Do	13/2/17 to 18/2/17		Guns fired during day and night at intervals onto dumps, roads, crossroads, tramways, and also deepened working parties.	
Do	19/2/17		During raid on right Brigade area, put a barrage across left flank of area raided.	
Do	20/2/17 to 28/2/17		Guns fired during day and night onto roads, dumps, tramways, crossroads and dispersed several working parties.	

A Macdull Lieut
O.C. 49 M.G. Coy

WAR DIARY
FOR MONTH OF MARCH, 1917.

VOLUME 12

UNIT:- 10th Machine Gun Company

Vol XI

Army Form C. 2118.

WAR DIARY
or
INTELLIGENCE SUMMARY
(Erase heading not required.)

49 Coy. M.G.C.

Instructions regarding War Diaries and Intelligence Summaries are contained in F. S. Regs., Part II. and the Staff Manual respectively. Title Pages will be prepared in manuscript.

Place	Date	Hour	Summary of Events and Information	Remarks and references to Appendices
WYTSCHAETE SECTOR	1/3/17		During raid by units of 47th Infty. Bde. gun fired onto BOGEART FARM O.25.a.99.99. HOP POINT N 30.d 80.80. BONE POINT N.36.b. 70.90	
Do.	2/3/17 to 7/3/17		Guns fired during hours of darkness onto Roads in O.31.a. O.19.d. N.36.b. O.31.c. on which according to photographic plant was movement.	
Do.	8/3/17	3.30 pm	Enemy opened a bombardment onto our left front about N.23.d 80.30 to 80.99. All gun teams stood to and prepared for action. At 5.10 pm the SOS was received for runners and all guns opened on their barrage lines (Appendix) The Fort was reinforced from the HQ at Kemmel and two extra guns were pushed into YONGE ST. HQ's was also transferred to temporary battle HQ in Yonge St. Shortly after the SOS came through. It was reported that enemy had entered our line about Broadway and that a defensive flank was being formed on VIA GELLIA. Therefore another gun was brought from Farm D'Home on our right into alternate position on Via Gellia. The emplacement S.I. in VIAGELLIA was hit, therefore the gun was retired to an alternate emplacement lower down the trench and came into action again. It was reported that the enemy was moving behind MAEDELSTEDE for an attack, therefore fire from 7 guns was applied to this target, no attack materialised. During the action our gun positions were very heavily shelled and the gunners showed great coolness in keeping up rapid fire throughout. After reinforcement had been pushed up more guns were firing into the sector attacked, in addition to the barrage behind the lines from the forts. The action closed about 8 pm.	
Do.	9/3/17	4.0 am	Enemy opened a bombardment and the SOS went up from about the head of VIA GELLIA and the GLORY HOLE. Barrage fire was instantly applied and kept up until the situation became normal. During the action the enemy artillery searched for all our left gun positions, one team being buried and two guns slightly damaged. These two guns were fired & the company had 6 cannelees during these two actions 81,000 rounds	
Do.	9/3/17 10/3/17		During night defended gap in front line with sweeping fire	

Army Form C. 2118.

WAR DIARY
or
INTELLIGENCE SUMMARY
(Erase heading not required.)

49 Comp. M.G.C.

Place	Date	Hour	Summary of Events and Information	Remarks and references to Appendices
WYTSCHAETE SECTOR	10/3/17		Enemy reported mass'ing behind WABBELSTETE and PETIT BOIS. Our Machinen Gun Barrage opened & fire opened by our guns, attack did not materialise.	
	11/3/17			
DO	12/3/17		Billets shelled. 4 casualties.	
	13/3/17		Company relieved by 109 M.G. Comp relief complete by 2 p.m. Comp. moved from Kemmel to SCHERPENBERG.	
	14/3/17		Cleaning guns & material. Wytschaete Sector held by 124 M.G.C.	
	15/3/17		Packing Limbers. Inspected sector held by 48 M.G.C.	
	16/3/17		Inspected sector held by 45 M.G.C. & billets at PIONEER FARM.	
	17/3/17		Packing limbers.	
VIERSTRAAT SECTOR	18/3/17		Relieved 45 M.G.C. in the VIERSTRAAT SECTOR. Took over billets at PIONEER FARM. G.O.C's inspection.	
	19/3/17 to 31/3/17		Reorganisation of all M.G. positions in the line, making 16 new recent positions on the VIERSTRAAT SWITCH. Laid down new Barrage lines & occasionally fired during night on enrage lines.	

A. Bracewell Lieut.
for O.C. 49 M.G. Co.

WAR DIARY FOR MONTH OF APRIL, 1917.

VOLUME:- 13

UNIT:- 49th Machine Gun Company

WAR DIARY
or
INTELLIGENCE SUMMARY

Army Form C. 2118.

49 Coy. Machine Gun Corps

Place	Date	Hour	Summary of Events and Information	Remarks and references to Appendices
VIERSTRAAT SECTOR	1/4/17		All guns and men in the line were relieved by 47 M.G.C. H.Q being also removed from PIONEER FARM N15.a.10.10 to KLONDYKE FARM M.24.d.95.30. being now in Brigade support.	
do	2/4/17 to 3/4/17		Repairing near billets, making beds, cleaning all guns and material.	
do	4/4/17		Firing guns on range during practice with Cloud and Shell gas, commenced classes in map reading, rangefinding	
do	5/4/17 to 8/4/17		Training programme carried out: gun drill, advanced training, classes in map reading, scouting, rangefinding, first aid, transport work, belt-filling and indirect fire	
do	9/4/17		Firing on 25 yds. range. Part I table. Cleaning old limber transferring same.	
do	10/4/17		Inspection of the company, guns & limbers at LOCRE by II Army Commander Gen. Plumer	
do	11/4/17 to 12/4/17		Training programme continued.	
RECQUES AREA	13/4/17 to 15/4/17		Marching to Training area at NORDAUSQUES. Reference map HAZEBROUCK Sheet 5.a. 1/100,000 Route BAILLEUL. HAZEBROUCK. ARQUES, ST.OMER. RECQUES.	
do	16/4/17 to 27/4/17		Training including field work, consolidation, advanced drill, wood fighting. Range practice. A field day in conjunction with the 49 Infty Bde in an instructional attack on the WYTSCHAETE RIDGE in which 8 guns were detached from Company for attachment to Infantry and 8 guns detailed for barrage fire on the various objectives.	
do	28/4/17 to 30/4/17		Marching from Training area to the LOCRE AREA inspected by Army Corps Commander Gen Hamilton Gordon on march through BAILLEUL. encamped on the night 30/4/17 - 1/5/17 at SCHERPENBERG M.17.B.30.40	

WAR DIARY:
--------oOo--------

VOLUME:- 14

FOR MONTH OF MAY, 1917.

UNIT:- 49th Machine Gun Company

Army Form C. 2118.

WAR DIARY
or
INTELLIGENCE SUMMARY

(Erase heading not required.)

49 Coy. M.G.C.

Instructions regarding War Diaries and Intelligence Summaries are contained in F.S. Regs., Part II. and the Staff Manual respectively. Title Pages will be prepared in manuscript.

Place	Date	Hour	Summary of Events and Information	Remarks and references to Appendices
DIEPENDAAL SECTOR	1/5/17		Relieved the 56th Coy. M.G.C. in the DIEPENDAAL Sector. Placing 4 guns in the line, NEW RESERVE and BREASTWORK N.6, 11 and 12. H.Q. removed from SCHERPENBERG to N.7.a.80.60.	
do	2/5/17 to 9/5/17		This afforded during hours of darkness into Enemy dumps, Supply Tramways, Barrage lines and lines of approach. Enemy front and NO MANS LAND, experimental bursts fired on the 7/5/17 billets were shelled, two men wounded.	
do	9/5/17		Enemy opened heavy bombardment on our front. S.O.S. signal was sent up at 9-10 p.m. Barrage fire instantly applied on barrage lines, no infantry attack materialised. 30,000 rds. were fired. Gun positions were heavily shelled, reinforcements were sent up from H.Q. but were not required.	
do	10/5/17		Relieved by the 56th Coy. M.G.C. This unit in turn relieved the 47 M.G.C. in the VIERSTRAAT SECTOR 12 guns being placed in the line in N.17, 16, 23 & 22. H.Q. removed to Pioneer Farm. N.15.a.00.10.	
VIERSTRAAT SECTOR	10/5/17 to 17/5/17		This afforded during hours of darkness onto gaps in wire made by artillery. Tramways, Trench junctions, Block pts., Hospice, and Woods	
do	18/5/17		Relieved by the 48 M.G.C. H.Q. removed to KLONDYKE FARM N.17.c.0.15.	
do	18/5/17 to 31/5/17		Commenced and completed preparations for the offensive. Attack on the WYTSCHAETE RIDGE. Belt filling depots & shelter built near PARRET FM. N.17a. to 48 M.G.C. & stocked with S.A.A. for 8 gun groups. do do built in SHANTUNG, CHINESE WALL, N.17B&d. for this unit for 10 gun groups. do do built adjacent to TAT ROAD & CHINESE WALL N.23.B. to 47 M.G.C. for 10 gun groups, all ammunition stocked with S.A.A. Material drawn & delivered for similar work to 33 Coy. & 48 Coy. Shelter near forward dumps constructed in N.17.a and N.17.B stocked with S.A.A. for this unit. Range chart, barrage fire lifts drawn up, special tracks for guns, water troughs, tramways made prepared for all coys. at 49.48.47.33 in Guns arranged for barrage fire during the attack are 49 Coy. 10 guns, 48 " 10 " (H. Halifax: Panet, Ankerie) 48 Coys 16 " (Calgary) 33 Coys 8 "	
			Six guns of this unit are detailed to go forward with attacking infantry	2 gns R High Regt. 2 " 9th R Irish Rgn. 2 " 7/8 R Irish Fusrs (cont)

2449 (Wt. W14957/M90 750,000 1/16 J.B.C. B.C. & A. Forms/C.2118/12.

Army Form C. 2118.

2

WAR DIARY
or
INTELLIGENCE SUMMARY

49 Coy. M.G.C.

(Erase heading not required.)

Place	Date	Hour	Summary of Events and Information	Remarks and references to Appendices
VIERSTRAAT SECTOR.	5/17		During the month. Capt. J.M. Davidson attached to this unit was wounded. Lt. G. BENNISON 2/Lt. GUDGIN } belonging to this unit were evacuated sick.	
	18/5/17		Major R. LE BUTT was appointed A/D.M.G.O. for the coming offensive	

A Bracewell Lt.
O.T. 49 Coy. M.G.C.

WAR   DIARY.

FOR   MONTH   OF   JUNE,   1917.

VOLUME :- 15.

UNIT :- 10th Machine Gun Company

Vol 14

Army Form C. 2118.

WAR DIARY
or
INTELLIGENCE SUMMARY
(Erase heading not required.)

49 Machine Gun Company

Instructions regarding War Diaries and Intelligence Summaries are contained in F. S. Regs., Part II. and the Staff Manual respectively. Title Pages will be prepared in manuscript.

Place	Date	Hour	Summary of Events and Information	Remarks and references to Appendices
KLONDYKE 7^N	1/6/17	7.0 pm	Working parties sent to the line, material for splinter proof shelters taken in. Ammunition supply increased by 5000 rounds.	
"	2/6/17	9.0 am	Relieved 48 M.G. Coy in the VIERSTRAAT SECTOR. 6 guns placed in line. Removed H.Q. to PIONEER R7M.	
In the line VIERSTRAAT AREA	3/6/17		Guns fired on barrage lines - UNNAMED WOOD - 2 guns taken up to Battery positions and lifts tested - 5000 rounds	
"	4/6/17		During night our troops gave attention to BOIS de WYTSCHAETE, UNNAMED WOOD, PETIT BOIS etc. Guns fired 13,000 rounds on the area being so treated.	
"	5/6/17		During night fired 20000 rds. on NAIL SWITCH, NAIL DRIVE	
"	6/6/17		Final preparations - all guns tested on barrage lines whilst artillery was active.	
"	7/6/17 to 10/6/17		Special reports attached for detail of operations. On night 7/8-6/17 Lt BRACEWELL, Lt BELLAMY, Lt MAY and 217 SIMPKINS was wounded.	
LOCRE AREA	11/6/17		Company left the line at 6.0 pm and returned to LOCRE AREA to rest	
"	12/6/17		All fighting limbers checked and prepared for emergency - Camp moved 100 yards.	
"	13/6/17	6.30 am	Marched to MERRIS Q REA - 33 reinforcements arrived	

McNeill

Army Form C. 2118.

WAR DIARY
or
INTELLIGENCE SUMMARY
(Erase heading not required.)

49 M.G. Coy.

Instructions regarding War Diaries and Intelligence Summaries are contained in F.S. Regs., Part II. and the Staff Manual respectively. Title Pages will be prepared in manuscript.

Place	Date	Hour	Summary of Events and Information	Remarks and references to Appendices
MERRIS	14/6/17	9.00am	Packing limbers, general overhaul of material and preparations for re-equipment begun	
"	15/6/17	7.00am	Baths, cleaning new equipment, re-clothing and general clean up - 4 Officer reinforcements arrived from Base	
"	16/6/17	10 am	Inspection by C.O.	
LOCRE AREA	17/6/17	5.30am	Company marched back to CLARE CAMP - LOCRE AREA	
"	18/6/17	4.45am	Company marched back to MERRIS AREA	
MERRIS	19/6/17	9.00am	Rebuilt camp. Latrines dug - clothing house erected - ablution places made.	
"	20/6/17	9.00am	Men's equipment shipped, thorough overhaul and cleaned up	
		2.30pm	Inspection and address by G.O.C. 49th Infantry Brigade.	
"	21/6/17	5.25am	Company moved to EECKE AREA	
EECKE AREA	22/6/17	5.10am	Company marched to BUYSSCHEURE AREA	
BUYSSCHEURE AREA	23/6/17	9.0am	Started latrines - ablution places and general sanitation of new camp.	
		5.0pm	Company moved to new billets in BUYSSCHEURE AREA	
"	24/6/17	7.00am	Programme of training started as per attached schedule.	

Army Form C. 2118.

WAR DIARY
or
INTELLIGENCE SUMMARY
(Erase heading not required.)

49 M.G. Coy

Instructions regarding War Diaries and Intelligence Summaries are contained in F.S. Regs., Part II. and the Staff Manual respectively. Title Pages will be prepared in manuscript.

Place	Date	Hour	Summary of Events and Information	Remarks and references to Appendices
BUYSSCHEURE	23/6/17 to 28/6/17	7.0am	Training carried on	
"	29/6/17	9.0am	Inspection by G.O.C. Division.	
"	30/6/17	6.0am	Moved to TILQUES training area	

R. Pickitt Major
O.C. 49 M.G. Co.

Time	June 24th (1st day)	June 25th (2nd day)	June 26th (3rd day)	June 27th (4th day)	June 28th (5th day)	June 29th (6th day)	June 30th (7th day)
6·0 am.	Reveille	Reveille	Reveille	Reveille	Reveille	Reveille	Reveille
7·0 am.	Squad Drill	Squad Drill	Squad Drill	Squad Drill	Squad Drill	Squad Drill	Squad Drill
9·0 am to 10·0 am.	Mechanism.	Gun Drill	Lecture on M.G.'s in village fighting (Carrying enemy's fire) (defence of Infantry)	Practice: bringing gun, tripods and ammunition on pack mule (Special carriers)	Examination of spare parts boxes.	Under Section Officers	Reveille tripods, etc carrying guns, Route March
10·0 am to 11·0 am.	Aiming instruction (particular attention will be paid to "laying" with mod 6 sights.)	Lecture on M.G.'s in fire- (a) Use of cover (b) Ammunition supply (c) Keeping communication	Practical instruction - modes of advance and traversing dial. (flank) M.G.s giving fire positions (close-co-ordinating for barrage work)	Lecture: co-operation with infantry in advance (Co-ordinating positions) rapid construction of S.P's	Belt-filling - hand & machine.		
11·15 am to 12·0 noon	Lecture on "Attention to duties"	Practice: loading and unloading limbers to time (tests)	Stoppages	Under Section Officers (Section roll books checking (B))	Lecture Collaboration with Lewis guns when in close support.		
12·0 noon to 1·0 pm.	Practical lessons on mounts before driving & after.	Physical drill	Physical drill	Physical drill	Physical drill	Physical drill	
2-30 pm.		N.C.O.s class :- Map reading		N.C.O.s class :- Map reading		N.C.O.s Compass work	

Transport drill carried out daily, swift pack animals.
Daily riding classes for N.C.O.s and drivers.

REPORT ON OPERATIONS.
7-6-17

As D.M.G.O. for the 16th Division, having control of the guns of the 3 Coys of the Division, and 8 guns of the 33rd M.G Coy, I desire to give you my impressions for your consideration:-

I am fully convinced that the distribution of the guns and the method of applying fire was the correct one. Of the 56 guns employed 44 were used for barrage, & 12 for proceeding with the Infantry.

BARRAGE GUNS.

These were worked in pairs -

each pair having a splinter-proof shelter for belt-filling & stores. These shelters were erected near the selected gun positions & as far as was possible out of view of the enemy. The guns were placed in the open fields & a few hours before the attack a small splinter-proof was erected over the gun implacements. Each took roughly one hour to build, but they proved their worth, for a close examination proved that they saved the guns and teams from shrapnel.

All belt-filling shelters were filled with S.A.A., oil, and water some days beforehand, & the guns and tripods were brought up two nights previous, in order to avoid congestion which would naturally occur on the eve of battle. Thus on the night of the 8th the men were able to proceed to their allotted positions unhampered by material. They appreciated this and arrived there quite fresh.

At Zero all guns opened fire according to the barrage table, & continued until Zero plus 4 hours. At Zero plus 4-20 they moved forwards some to positions to continue a further barrage & some to strong points

All guns arrived at their allotted positions well up to time.

Mule stations were built well forward with stores of S.A.A.; also water for guns and men. The latter most important. Limbers full of ammunition and water were kept at points known to all gunners, ready to be pushed forward. At a given signal all pack mules & limbers moved forward to a rendezvous, guided by the supply officer, whose duty it was to reconnoitre the country & push forward supplies at the earliest possible moment. The M.G mules arrived at their advanced

posts one hour before the infantry transport.
For future operations of a similar nature
9 insiders one Officer per Company.
should be selected for this work. The
success of the M.G.'s was due in no small
measure to communication — both
telephones and runners, which worked
splendidly. At no time from Zero
to Zero plus 12 hours was I out of
touch with any Coy. When the
ground permitted communication was
retained by telephone. Casualties
were thus replaced with great rapidity
guns & teams directed to their correct
position & supplies kept up.

Batt'n Comm'rs and many other infantry officers are most enthusiastic in expressing their appreciation of the M.G. work — Platoon Comm'rs particularly. They consider it gave their men great confidence & not one had any complaint to make of bullets falling short. It is impossible to get a correct figure of the number of rounds fired, but 900,000 is within the figure! One German prisoner who spoke English, when I asked him if the artillery fire was terrible replied: "Terrible — & the Machine-Gun!" I have made a careful examination of certain portion of the ground where the barrage was playing, & found dead men & horses, telegraph poles & trees riddled with bullets.

Too much work cannot be devoted to the preliminary — nothing must be left to chance, and obstacle which might arise must be considered.

Officers & men worked very hard, transport personnel were thoroughly trained, & did their work well, many gun teams at 5 p.m. sitting down to a hot meal the other side of the Ridge. Water for the men in these attacks is an important thing — the dust & fumes seem to give them an unquenchable thirst.

GUNS WITH INFANTRY

The guns that went with Battalions in one or two instances went rather astray - principally through the explosion of the mines.

They were eventually got together by the N.C.O's and reached their allotted posts with little delay.

REPORT on OPERATIONS OF M Gs AT MAUVE LINE FROM THE TIME OF LEAVING THE HOSPICE TILL BEING RELIEVE BY THE 33rd M.G. Coy.

At Zero plus 6-30 I left the HOSPICE RIDGE with 4 guns, two of which were taken by Lt Bellamy and the remaining two Stork to a point behind the MAUVE LINE at O.20d.60.50. to support the attack of the 33rd Inf. Bde. On seeing this Brigad leave their position for the attack I opened up barrage fire at a point 300x beyond the ODONTO LINE for a period of 10 minutes when I ceased fire, oiled up, and refilled belts and laid my gun on the

S.O.S Line

I remained in position until the objective was taken and the guns of the 33rd M.G. Coy were in position. I then returned to the HOSPICE

REPORT on OPERATIONS.   "C" SECT
                        7-6-17

As Officer i/c. of 2 guns attached to 2nd Bn. Irish Regt. Stook up my position at HORLEY, until Zero plus one hour, when I moved up and attached myself to the support Coy ("B" Coy) 2nd R.I. Regt. At Zero plus 2 hours all moved up to the BLUE LINE, stopping at the arranged position. At 3.10 the Batt. started the attack on the BLACK LINE, our two guns following up with the Support Coy. No opposition was found at all. Believing that the Batt. had gone a bit too far, I followed them up and took up a position in the copse at O.20.a.70.24. No sign of the enemy at all was seen. The guns however fired 500 rounds on S.O.S. Line beyond ODONTO trench. On discovering that the 2nd Bn. T Regt occupied the BLACK LINE, I took up my allotted position about O.20.a.10.60. About mid-day the following day the Section went out to FORT HALIFAX. No casualties of any description.

REPORT ON OPERATIONS   "C" Sect
                        7-6-17

At Zero plus 30 minutes I went to Coy. H.Q. in Chinese Wall & met Lieut Pascoe who informed me that Lt Bracewell & Simpkins had been wounded, also that as he was taking over command of the Coy would I take over his two guns & Lt Simpkins fours, which I did

At Zero plus 4-20 we left our positions on Chinese Wall & advanced to the HOSPICE RIDGE, I placed the ten guns on a line running from O.19.a.60.90. to O.13.c.60.40. These guns continued the Barrage until Zero plus 6.30, when Lieut Jefferies Ferward with 4 guns to take up positions in the MAUVE LINE. He was subsequently relieved by the 33rd M.G. Coy. The remaining six guns continued Barrage fire until Zero plus 10 hours when they ceased fire as per orders.

Meanwhile Lt Pascoe had established Coy H.Q. in UNNAMED WOOD at O.13.6. 15.40 and was in telephone communication with D.M.G.O. Orders were then received to place guns in such a position as to defend the RIDGE. For this purpose 5 guns K. a lie O13.c.80.10 to O13.c.80.

Two Guns "E" Sect arrived about Zero plus 11.30 & were placed in position and were placed just in rear of these five guns & given indirect lines of fire for barrage if necessary.

Lieut Turner had established a S.A.A. dump in a shell hole about O 13.c.50.0 from from which my guns drew their requirements

Lieut Pascoe was relieved on the 6th inst. about 4 pm

One gun was placed in a position about in a SP near RED CHATEAU at 013C.107

I was relieved by Lt McQueen and 7 gun teams and withdrew to FORT HALIFAX about 12 midday on the 9' inst, taking out 7 gun teams while one remained behind.

REPORT ON OPERATIONS   7-6-17

The Coy had 10 guns in shelters at CHINESE WALL, 4 under Lt Simpkins, 2 under Lt Pascoe, 2 under Lt Collinson & 2 with Lt Joyce. O.C. Coy, Lt Bracewell had his HQ at CHINESE WALL.

At Zero hour all these guns opened fire as per barrage programme. At Zero plus 30 mins Lt Bracewell & Lt Simpkins were both wounded. I immediately took over the duties of O.C. Company & got into telephonic communication with O.M.G.O.   Lt Collinson &

Joyce supervised the guns.

All guns fired as per programme up to Zero plus 4 hours. We had no stoppages or trouble with any of these guns.

At Zero plus 4.20. these guns were carried forward to the HOSPICE LINE, took up positions and continued barrage fire until Zero plus 6-30. At the same time I established HQ in UNNAMED WOOD at O.13 C 15. 40. The telephone was laid on within a few minutes & I got into communication with D.M.G.O.

"At Zero + 6.20 Lt Joyce moved forward with 4 guns to take up a position in the MAUVE LINE. Two of these guns were taken over by Lt Bellamy & the remaining two took up a position behind the MAUVE LINE at 0.20 & 60:50 to support the attack of the 33rd Inf Bde & opened up Barrage fire for 10 minutes then laid on to the S.O.S Line & remained in position until objective was taken & the guns of the 33rd M.G Coy were in position when they returned to the HOSPICE RIDGE.

The six guns remaining at the HOSPICE

RIDGE continued Barrage fire until Zero plus 10 hours when they ceased fire

Orders were received by O.M.G.S. to place guns in position to defend RIDGE - this was done - see report from "C" Section attached

At about Zero plus 11.30 two guns from "C" Section reported at HQ & were placed in position on the RIDGE

Lt Turner established a S.A.A. dump about O.13.c.50.0 from which all ammunition required was drawn I received orders for relief on the night of the 7th inst, but these orders were cancelled shortly after by Brigade, all guns remained in their positions.

I was relieved about 4 pm on the 8th June & handed over to Lt Green in accordance with instructions from OM GO

WAR DIARY.

FOR MONTH OF JULY, 1917.

VOLUME :- 16

UNIT :- 49th Machine Gun Compy

Army Form C. 2118.

WAR DIARY
or
INTELLIGENCE SUMMARY
(Erase heading not required.)

CONFIDENTIAL

War Diary of the 49th Company, Machine Gun Corps.

From 1st July 1917 — 31st July 1917 (inclusive)

[signature]
O.C. 49 M.G. Co.

Army Form C. 2118.

WAR DIARY
or
INTELLIGENCE SUMMARY

(Erase heading not required.)

4 9 M. G. COY

Instructions regarding War Diaries and Intelligence Summaries are contained in F.S. Regs., Part II and the Staff Manual respectively. Title Pages will be prepared in manuscript.

Place	Date	Hour	Summary of Events and Information	Remarks and references to Appendices
TATINGHEM	1/7/17		Church Parade.	Pte
	2/7/17		Range Practice - stoppages.	Pte
Ref. Map BELGIUM HAZEBROUCK 5A 1/100,000	3/7/17 - 5/7/17		Company training	Pte
	6/7/17		Brigade field day	Pte
	7/7/17		Brigade field day - Co-operation with Tanks	Pte
	8/7/17		Move to ROUBROUCK AREA	Pte
	9/7/17		Move to WINNEZEELE AREA	Pte
WINNIZEELE Ref. Map BELGIUM HAZEBROUCK 5A 1/100,000	10/7/17		Church Parade (Special Service) - Kit inspection and clean up	Pte
	11/7/17		Company training	Pte
	12/7/17		Generals' Inspection - Presentation of Divisional Parchments	Pte
	13/7/17 14/7/17		Company training	Pte
	15/7/17		Church Parade	Pte
	16/7/17 18/7/17		Company training	Pte
	19/7/17		Inter Section Competition - Men's turn out and transport	Pte

O.C. 49 M.G. Co.

Army Form C. 2118.

WAR DIARY
or
INTELLIGENCE SUMMARY

(Erase heading not required.)

49 M.G. Coy

Place	Date 1917	Hour	Summary of Events and Information	Remarks and references to Appendices
WINNEZEELE	20/7/17		Brigade Inspection – by Divisional General	Nil
Ref: map BELGIUM HAZEBROUCK 5A 1/100,000	21/7/17		Demonstration of using pack Saddlery. Sections practised.	Nil
	22/7/17		Church Parade – afternoon :- Brigade Tactical scheme.	Nil
	23/7/17		Demonstration of M.G's :- open warfare – The advance – Staff Supervision.	Nil
	24/7/17		Tactical Scheme – afternoon :- Cleaning limbers	Nil
	25/7/17		Wet day. Lecture in morning. afternoon : work on limbers – 109 MG.Coy take over camp.	Nil
	26/7/17		Moved to No 2 WATOU AREA	Nil
WATOU (area no. 2.) Ref: map BELGIUM HAZEBROUCK 5A 1/100,000	27/7/17		Gas helmet inspection – non ration inspection. Capt K.S. MASON arrives and takes over Coy.	Nil
	28/7/17		Inspection of Coy by C.O.	Nil
	29/7/17		Wet day	Nil
	30/7/17		Prepared to move – 11.30 pm move to BEDOUIN CAMP	Nil
	31/7/17		All fighting limbers overhauled – Coy pay out. rest.	Nil

O.C. 49 M.G. Coy.

WAR DIARY.

FOR MONTH OF AUGUST, 1917.

VOLUME...17...

UNIT 49th Machine Gun Company.

Army Form C. 2118

WAR DIARY
or
INTELLIGENCE SUMMARY
(Erase heading not required.)

WAR DIARY
OF THE
49TH. MACHINE GUN COMPANY
FOR
AUGUST 1917.

Army Form C. 2118.

WAR DIARY
or
INTELLIGENCE SUMMARY

(Erase heading not required.)

Instructions regarding War Diaries and Intelligence Summaries are contained in F. S. Regs., Part II. and the Staff Manual respectively. Title pages will be prepared in manuscript.

Hour, Date, Place	Summary of Events and Information	Remarks and references to Appendices
9 p.m. 1/8/17 BEDOUIN CAMP Sheet 28. N.W. G.6.B.60.30.	The Coy paraded to move off to the forward area in the vicinity of VLAMERTINGHE & placed under 2 hrs notice to move into the line.	L.M.C.
10 a.m. 2/8/17 VLAMERTINGHE.	The Coy moves back to BEDOUIN CAMP.	L.M.C.
4 a.m. 3/8/17 BEDOUIN CAMP	The line was reconnoitred by the C.O. & two other officers	L.M.C.
6 p.m.	The Coy moves into the line. The following positions were taken over by map ref. 28 N.E. 6 guns of 46 M.G. Coy were relieved - 4 guns in vicinity of SQUARE FARM. 4 guns of the "B" Coy from position in vicinity of FREZENBERG CROSS ROADS. Coy Hdqrs established at MILLCOT. 1 Section in Ruins at the RAMPARTS YPRES.	L.M.C.
11.30 p.m.	Relief complete. Casualties 1 wounded	
4/8/17 MILL COT.	Situation normal. SQUARE FARM position shelled during the day	L.M.C.
5/8/17 " do "	Situation same	L.M.C.
6/8/17 " do "	Situation normal. Enemy aircraft active	L.M.C.
9 p.m. 7/8/17 " do "	Intre Coy relief took place. 4 guns from SQUARE FARM withdrawn to old German front line in vicinity of STABLES.	L.M.C.
3.45 p.m. 8/8/17 " do "	Situation normal. Enemy aircraft active	L.M.C.
3 p.m. 9/8/17	Situation unchanged. Enemy aeroplane flying low. In evening at 9 p.m. an S.O.S signal was observed. Our line was opened & maintained until the all clear signal was given. The slackened off well the activity	L.M.C.

Army Form C. 2118.

WAR DIARY
or
INTELLIGENCE SUMMARY.
(Erase heading not required.)

Instructions regarding War Diaries and Intelligence Summaries are contained in F.S. Regs., Part II. and the Staff Manual respectively. Title pages will be prepared in manuscript.

Place	Date	Hour	Summary of Events and Information	Remarks and references to Appendices
MILL COT	10/8/17		Situation normal.	
"	10/8/17	1pm	4 guns relieved at SQUARE FARM by 225 Coy. 4 guns at FREZENBERG CROSS ROADS by the same Coy. These two Sections withdrew to Transport Lines Ref Sheet 28 N.W. H.16.0.5.4.	ZMC ZMC
Coy Hdg H.16.0.5.4	11/8/17		Section at Stables (old gun shot hm) came under orders of O.C. 225 Coy	ZMC
"	12/8/17	4.30am	S.O.S. went up. Fire opened & maintained for about ¾ hour.	ZMC
"		7pm	Between the Section at the "Stables" relieved by 4 M.G. Coy. Section withdrew to Transport Lines H.16.0.5.4.	ZMC
"	13/8/17		In camp at H.16.0.5.4.	ZMC
MILL COT	14/8/17 11.30pm		One Section relieved 225 Coy at SQUARE FARM. One Section relieved 225 Coy at FREZENBERG CROSS R⁴	ZMC
"	15/8/17 10pm		One other Section arrived at SQUARE FARM. One Section moved to horselines at Stables	ZMC

WAR DIARY
INTELLIGENCE SUMMARY
(Erase heading not required.)

Army Form C. 2118

Place	Date	Hour	Summary of Events and Information	Remarks and references to Appendices
MILL COT	16/8/17	4.45 a.m.	The disposal of the guns at Zero was as follows. Ref map FREZENBERG 1/10000. 8 guns on the vicinity of Square Fme. 4 guns in vicinity of FREZENBERG CROSS ROADS. 4 guns at Noble's old German front line. These four guns were to move forward later, the remaining 12 opened fire on their barrage line at Zero & continued firing as per programme until Zero + 150". Four guns dropped out at Q Farm at Zero + 35" as per programme & got ready to move forward to positions at IBERIAN FARM & BECK HOUSE when the artillery red line was captured – being consolidated. Owing to the nature of the operations these guns were again mounted & laid on the S.O.S. lines. The enemy barrage came down very heavily on the line of gun positions & one gun was knocked out three men were killed. During the morning the S.O.S. went up & all guns opened fire. After a time Germans were observed coming down the roads & nullahs & small parties, they were successfully engaged by direct fire. S.A.A. was obtained from a pack mule dump. During the operation the barrage guns fired approx. 160000 rounds. At Zero + 65" orders were issued to the Section – the old German front line to move forward to the following positions.	[illegible]

WAR DIARY
or
INTELLIGENCE SUMMARY
(Erase heading not required.)

Army Form C. 2118

Place	Date	Hour	Summary of Events and Information	Remarks and references to Appendices
HILL COT	16/8/17	2+ 65"	2 guns to DELVA FARM. These guns never reached their objective Hill 37, but got as far as IBERIAN FARM when they took up defensive positions where they came into action & covered the retirement of the Infantry. The casualties suffered by the Coy were as follows:- Officers 4, O.R. 41, Guns 4 complete.	ZWC
MILL COT	17/8/17	11 am	Quiet day. 8 guns still at Sg. FARM & 4 at FREZENBERG CROSS ROADS.	
		10 pm	These guns were relieved by 12 guns of 46" M.G. Coy & withdrew to Transport lines. Relief complete at 11 pm.	DWC
Coy Hdq. H16.D.5.4 SHEET 28 N.W.	18/8/17.	2 pm	Transport left for WATOU No II AREA. Coy embarked on motor busses at 5.30 at VLAMERTINGHE & proceed to WATOU No II area arriving in Camp about 8 pm.	ZWC
Coy Hdq K17.B.3.4.	19/8/17		Coy moved from Above Camp to new Bde Hdq at K17B 3.4 Sheet 27.	

Army Form C. 2118.

WAR DIARY
or
INTELLIGENCE SUMMARY

(Erase heading not required.)

Instructions regarding War Diaries and Intelligence Summaries are contained in F. S. Regs., Part II. and the Staff Manual respectively. Title pages will be prepared in manuscript.

Hour, Date, Place	Summary of Events and Information	Remarks and references to Appendices
Coy Hdqrs. 20/8/17 Godewaersveld	Coy marched to billets — GODEWAELWELD	JMC
2 p.m. 21/8/17	Coy marched to Caestre & entrained about 7.30 p.m.	JMC
4 a.m. 22/8/17	Coy arrived & detrained at MIRAUMONT & marched to ACHIET-LE-PETIT.	JMC
23/8/17	In Camp ACHIET-LE-PETIT	JMC
24/8/17	In Camp do.	JMC
25/8/17	Church Parade in ACHIET-LE-PETIT	JMC
26/8/17	In Camp. Line reconnoitred by Section Officers	JMC
27/8/17	Coy marched to HORONNEVILLE	JMC
28/8/17	Work on Camp at HORONNEVILLE. Detail officers reconnoitre the line	JMC
29/8/17	Work on Camp & roads at do	JMC
30/8/17	do do do	JMC
31/8/17	do do do	JMC

O.C. 49 M.G.C.

WAR   DIARY.

FOR MONTH OF SEPTEMBER, 1917.

VOLUME 18

UNIT:- M.G.C. 4gth Machine Gun Coy

WAR DIARY or INTELLIGENCE SUMMARY

Army Form C. 2118

Place	Date	Hour	Summary of Events and Information	Remarks and references to Appendices
MOYENNEVILLE	1/9/17	11 a.m.	In Camp. Church parade.	
"	2/9/17	12 noon	Two Sections of Coy relieved 1 Section 48 M.G. Co & 1 Section 47 M.G. Co	
"	3/9/17	9 a.m.	Situation - line normal. Sections working on emplacements & dugouts.	
"	4/9/17	"	Situation normal. New position sited at U 20 c 80.60. Ref map SHEET 51B S.W.4.	
"	5/9/17	10.30 p.m.	Teams shoot to during chemical shell bombardments. Very little retaliation.	
BUCQUOY	6/9/17	9.0 a.m.	Situation normal. Emplacements improved.	
"	7/9/17	noon	New position reconnoitred at junction of Nelly & Janet avenues. Ref map 51B. S.W.4.	
MAP REF	8/9/17	5.0 p.m.	C Section relieved A Section - lt Tin Situation normal	
	9/9/17	8.0 a.m.	1000 gas drums fired on on to German lines.	
		10 p.m.	Enemy retaliated on quarry & round CROISELLES with gas shells.	

WAR DIARY
or
INTELLIGENCE SUMMARY

Army Form C. 2118

(Erase heading not required.)

Place	Date	Hour	Summary of Events and Information	Remarks and references to Appendices
HAVRINCOURT	10/9/17	10 p.m.	Line reconnoitred by C.O. & D.M.G.O. Situation quiet.	HMC
	11/9/17		Situation quiet.	A
	12/9/17	5.30 p.m. 6.30 p.m.	QUARRY shelled. "II" Section relieved two guns of "I" Section in the QUARRY, two of 48 m.g. Coy. (L.F.2 and L.F.3). Otherwise situation normal.	A
	13/9/17	9.0 a.m.	Inter-company relief. 2000 rds. fired on Boche working parties. KNUCKLE AVE. shelled with 8" & 9" QUARRY shelled	Mu
	14/9/17		Situation quiet	Mu
	16/9/17			Mu
	17/9/17		A.A. gun at the QUARRY fired at hostile aircraft 2000 rds. fired at U.7.b.80.45 2500 " " Cross Rds v.15.b 2500 " " U.7.b.80.50 2500 " " U.14.a.30.70	Map ref. BULLECOURT 51.B S.W.4.

MAP REF. BULLECOURT 51.B.S.W.4.

WAR DIARY or INTELLIGENCE SUMMARY

Army Form C. 2118

Place	Date	Hour	Summary of Events and Information	Remarks and references to Appendices
NOYONNELLE	18/9/17	2.30 pm / 5.30 pm	4000 rds fired on OLDENBURG LANE in cooperation with heavy T.M.s. map ref BULLECOURT 51B S.W 4	
		8.0 pm / 4.30 am	2500 " " U7 b 8.5	do
			1500 " " U 14 a 5.7	do
		8.0 pm / 4.30 am	2500 " " CROSS Rds. U15 b	do
			KNUCKLE AVE / MANCHESTER RES / FACTORY } shelled during the day	do
	19/9/17	7.0 pm / 6.0 am	10000 rds fired on { U3 c 7.7 / U7 b 8.5 / U14 a 5.7 / CROSSRds U15 b	do
	20/9/17		Situation Quiet	do
	21/9/17	3.25 pm / 4.21 pm / 8.15 pm / 4.30 am	} 9000 rds fired on OLDENBURG LANE	do
		8.0 pm / 2.0 am	} 2500 rds fired on { U2 a 6.6 / U2 a 7.5	do
	22/9/17		Situation Quiet	do

Army Form C. 2118.

WAR DIARY
or
INTELLIGENCE SUMMARY
(Erase heading not required.)

Instructions regarding War Diaries and Intelligence Summaries are contained in F.S. Regs, Part II. and the Staff Manual respectively. Title Pages will be prepared in manuscript.

Place	Date	Hour	Summary of Events and Information	Remarks and references to Appendices
MOYENNEVILLE	23/9/17	8.0pm to 4.30am	2000 rds fired on U2a 6.6 to U2a 7.5 Map ref BULLECOURT 51 B S.W.4	(sig)
	24/9/17	9.00am	Enemy aeroplane engaged causing it to return over its own lines	(sig)
		8.0pm to 5.00am	2500 rds fired on U2a 6.6 to U2a 7.5	
		4.30am	1000 rds fired on S.O.S signals being set up. Heavy Bombardment just S. of positions and too misty to see any further signals	
	25/9/17	10.pm to 5.00am	2500 rds fired on U2a 6.6 to U2a 7.5 Map ref. BULLECOURT 51B S.W.4 Intersection relief carried out.	(sig)
MAP REF. BULLECOURT 51B S.W.4	26/9/17	3.0pm	Enemy aeroplane engaged	(sig)
		7.40pm to 4.0am	1500 rds fired on U7 b 8.5	
		9.15pm to 4.30am	1500 rds fired on U8 c 10.15	do
	27/9/17	8.15pm to 5.00am	2500 rds fired on U2a 6.6 to U2a 7.5	do

Army Form C. 2118.

WAR DIARY
or
INTELLIGENCE SUMMARY
(Erase heading not required.)

Instructions regarding War Diaries and Intelligence Summaries are contained in F. S. Regs., Part II. and the Staff Manual respectively. Title Pages will be prepared in manuscript.

Place	Date	Hour	Summary of Events and Information	Remarks and references to Appendices
MOYENNEVILLE	28/9/17	3.10pm to 4.30pm	2500 rds fired on U14 b 5.5 Map ref. BULLECOURT 51 B S.W.4	Ofle
			3000 " " " U 8 a 5١.52 do	
			2000 " " " U 7 a 85.80 do	
		9pm to 5am	2000 " " " O2 a 66 to O2 a 75 do	Ofle
	29/9/17	8.35pm to 5.30am	2000 rds. fired on O2 a 66 to O2 a 75 do	Ofle
	30/9/17		Situation quiet	

W Shu... Capt.
O.C. 49 M.O. Cd.

WAR DIARY

FOR MONTH OF OCTOBER, 1917.

UNIT 49th Machine Gun Company

VOLUME NUMBER 19

CONFIDENTIAL

War Diary of the 49th Machine Gun Coy. for October 1917

Army Form C. 2118.

WAR DIARY
or
INTELLIGENCE SUMMARY

(Erase heading not required.)

Instructions regarding War Diaries and Intelligence Summaries are contained in F. S. Regs., Part II. and the Staff Manual respectively. Title Pages will be prepared in manuscript.

Place	Date	Hour	Summary of Events and Information	Remarks and references to Appendices
MOYENNEVILLE	1/10/17		2000 rds fired on U 2 a 60.60	A.W.
	2/10/17		Shelter at junction of STAFFORD AVENUE & STRANGEWAYS blown in by heavy T.M. No Casualties. 2000 rds fired on U 8 a 28.68	A.W.
	3/10/17		2500 rds fired on U 8 a 28.68. Work carried on - dugouts, emplacements etc.	A.W.
	4/10/17		2600 rds fired on U 8 a 28.68. Situation quiet.	A.W.
	5/10/17		2500 rds fired on U 8 a 28.68. Work carried on - dugouts etc.	A.W.
	6/10/17		3000 rds fired on U 8 a 28.68 in cooperation with T.M. shoot. 2000 rds fired on U 8 a 28.68 during the night.	A.W.
	7/10/17		Eight guns cooperated with artillery at 5pm. 2000 rds fired on U 8 a 28.68	A.W.
	8/10/17		Light firing as usual. 2500 rounds being fired on U8a28.68.	A.W.
	9/10/17		M.G. coop-ated with T.M.'s in th afternoon, 2000 rounds fired on U8a 28.68.	T.M.C A.W.

Map Reference BULLECOURT 51B S.W.4

Army Form C. 2118.

WAR DIARY
or
INTELLIGENCE SUMMARY

(Erase heading not required.)

Instructions regarding War Diaries and Intelligence Summaries are contained in F. S. Regs., Part II. and the Staff Manual respectively. Title Pages will be prepared in manuscript.

Place	Date	Hour	Summary of Events and Information	Remarks and references to Appendices
MOYENNEVILLE	10/10/17		4000 rds. fired on V3c 20 70 Situation very quiet	
	11/10/17		2500 rds fired on U8a 28 68 Work continued on dug outs, emplacements etc. Enemy aircraft fired on 500 rds fired	
	12/10/17	8.10pm	500 rds fired on U21a 70 55	
		11pm	2800 rds fired on V14 d 00 70	
	13/10/17		4000 rds fired on OLDENBURG LANE work continued Situation Quiet	
	14/10/17		B & D Company relief	
	15/10/17		No firing Much work on dugouts and emplacements started Work continues	
	16/10/17		2000 rds on V14 a 95 50 4500 rds on V14 a 95 50 10,000 rds on TUNNEL TRENCH This was done whilst a small raid was carried out by adjoining Brigade	

Map Reference
BULLECOURT 51 b S.E. 4

WAR DIARY or INTELLIGENCE SUMMARY

Army Form C. 2118.

(Erase heading not required.)

Place	Date	Hour	Summary of Events and Information	Remarks and references to Appendices
MOYENNEVILLE	17/10/17		2000 rds fired on U.14.a.95.50 Work on dugouts, emplacements etc carried on	Ack
	16/10/17		Enemy aircraft fired on 250 rds. Work on dugouts, emplacements etc carried on 1500 rds. fired on U.8.b.75.50 Positions 46 & 47 shelled at 9.30 am & 9.0 pm 1500 rds " " U.8.c.95.95 Positions 43 & 44 " at 3.0 pm & 9.0 pm with 2500 rds " " V.3.a.00.60 Shrapnel 9.4.25	Ack
	19/10/17		2500 rds fired on U.8.C.30.35 10.p.m. 46 & 47 positions shelled with shrapnel 1500 rds " " U.8.c.95.95 10.30pm 43 & 44 " " 1500 rds " " U.8.b.75.50 Work continued 250 rds " " U.7.b.75.45 (light T.M.)	Ack
	20/10/17		1500 rds fired on U.8.b.75.50 FACTORY shelled 7.30–11.0 pm 12 5.9's 1500 rds " " U.8.C.95.95 Work Continued Harris dugout at 42 A Right by 4 2	Ack
	21/10/17		2000 rds. fired on U.8.b.75.50 The QUARRY intermittently shelled with 2000 rds " " U.8.C.95.95 gas shells. 1500 rds. fired at Enemy aircraft. 70? ALLEY shelled with 77 m shells Work on dugouts etc continued	Ack

	22/10/17	12 noon	We cooperated with a successful daylight raid on the enemy trenches. The following
			targets were engaged:— 3000 rds fired on U.14.a. 85.65 1500 rds fired on U.7.b. 80.30
			                         2000 rds " " U.7.d. 85.10 2500 " " U.1.c. 70.20
			                         1500 rds " " U.14.a. 10.70 2800 " " U.8.a. 20.55
			                                                    3000 " " U.8.a. 10.10
				Ack

Map Reference
BULLECOURT 51B S.W. 4.

WAR DIARY
or
INTELLIGENCE SUMMARY

(Erase heading not required.)

Army Form C. 2118.

Instructions regarding War Diaries and Intelligence Summaries are contained in F. S. Regs., Part II. and the Staff Manual respectively. Title Pages will be prepared in manuscript.

Place	Date	Hour	Summary of Events and Information	Remarks and references to Appendices
MOYENNEVILLE	22/10/17 (contd)		Work was continued on Anyork's Emplacements etc. FACTORY was shelled between 8 pm and 9 pm with about 30 shells nearly all of which were duds.	
			43944 positions shelled with 12 5.9 s	
			46747 " " " 4 4.2 s	
			70 PLANE " " " 4 4.2 s	
	23/9/17		2500 rds fired on V2A 90.60 Work was continued on dugouts & emplacements etc.	
			3000 " " " V2d 00.10	
	24/10/17		FACTORY shelled about 8.38pm with 20.v.9s. Enemy M.Gs abnormally active during the night.	
			8000 rds fired on V3c 20.70. Situation very quiet.	
			Positions 41. A (1) 941 A (2) were searched (by enemy M.G)	
	25/10/17 12:45 to 1:30pm		5000 rds fired on V8d 10.15 ⎫ in cooperation with artillery & T.M.S. 20.4.4mm shells burst a few yards to the right of position 4.3	
			5000 " " " TUNNEL TRENCH ⎬	
			2250 " " " V3c 20.70 ⎬	
			4500 " " " V9d 90.85 ⎭ Enemy M.Gs very quiet.	
	26/10/17		Work continued on emplacements, dugouts etc. No firing done. Situation abnormally quiet.	

Map Reference
BULLECOURT 51B S.W. 4

WAR DIARY
or
INTELLIGENCE SUMMARY

(Erase heading not required.)

Army Form C. 2118.

Place	Date	Hour	Summary of Events and Information	Remarks and references to Appendices
MOYENNEVILLE	27/10/17		4000 rds fired on H.Q. at U2a 70.60 4500 " " " U2d 0015 6000 " enfilading FAG ALLEY 3750 " " on U14a 2070 4250 " " " U7d 65.10 4000 " " " U7d 65.35 4250 " " enfilading U7d 60.80 15000 " " enfilading OLDENBURG LANE Hostile M.G's normal 20 S.9.6 fell in the vicinity of the FACTORY 20 .77mms fell in vicinity of 43&44 positions	In cooperation with Smoke and Gas bombardments at 10pm 26th and 9.3 am 27th inst.
	28/10/17		3000 rds fired enfilading TUNNEL TRENCH 3000 rds fired on U14d 3070 5000 rds fired enfilading OLDENBURG LANE 2250 rds fired on U14a 4095 12 Enemy were seen in U9d and engaged from POM ALLEY. They dispersed hurriedly but range was too great to see if any were casualties. 43 position shelled with 77mm shells FACTORY fired on with enemy M.G.	Work carried on as usual In conjunction with artillery concentration 3.10pm to 3.55pm
BULLECOURT SIEGE	29/10/17		CONCRETE TRENCH and SHAFT TRENCH shelled with 4.2s. Situation very quiet until 4.45pm when we raided enemy trenches	

Map reference

Army Form C. 2118.

WAR DIARY
or
INTELLIGENCE SUMMARY
(Erase heading not required.)

Instructions regarding War Diaries and Intelligence Summaries are contained in F. S. Regs., Part II and the Staff Manual respectively. Title Pages will be prepared in manuscript.

Place	Date	Hour	Summary of Events and Information	Remarks and references to Appendices
MOYENNEVILLE S.14	29/10/17	4.45 p.m	17,000 rds fired on the following targets: U.7.b 80.90, U.7.b 70-70, U.7.d 80.85, U.7.d 90.60, U.7.d 95.35, U.8.c 05.15. During the raid at 4.45 p.m	(1)
			Enemy artillery active between 5-6 p.m on SHAFT TRENCH & 70 PLANE. Work carried on as usual.	
BULLECOURT S13 S.14	30/10/17		½ Company relief. Company relieved in the line by 47 M.G. Coy.	(2)
	31/10/17		Cleaning up Baths etc.	(3)

J. Thomas
a/O.C. 49 M.G. Coy

Map Reference

WAR DIARY

FOR MONTH OF NOVEMBER, 1917.

VOLUME:- 20

UNIT:- Hq. Machine Gun Coy

Army Form C. 2118.

WAR DIARY
or
INTELLIGENCE SUMMARY.

(Erase heading not required.)

Instructions regarding War Diaries and Intelligence Summaries are contained in F. S. Regs., Part II. and the Staff Manual respectively. Title pages will be prepared in manuscript.

Place	Date	Hour	Summary of Events and Information	Remarks and references to Appendices
			CONFIDENTIAL. WAR DIARY OF THE 49TH MACHINE GUN COY. FOR NOVEMBER 1917.	

Army Form C. 2118.

WAR DIARY
or
INTELLIGENCE SUMMARY

(Erase heading not required.)

Instructions regarding War Diaries and Intelligence Summaries are contained in F.S. Regs., Part II. and the Staff Manual respectively. Title Pages will be prepared in manuscript.

Place	Date	Hour	Summary of Events and Information	Remarks and references to Appendices
MOYENNEVILLE	1/11/16	8.45am	Programme of work started. Inspection by O.C. Guns, spare parts cleaned – inspected by O.C. Physical Training. Mechanism and Gun drill. Recreational training.	Boots, clothing etc. attended to. Work on camp carried on. Tables for mens messes, fireplaces etc. put in hand.
	2/11/16	8.45am	Inspection by O.C. Revolver practice. Physical training. Instruction in map reading. Recreational Training.	Work on camp proceeded with.
	3/11/16	8.45am	Inspection by O.C. Revolver practice. Physical Training. Lecture on "Indirect Barrage Fire". Recreational Training.	Work on camp proceeded with. Brick stand for water cart built. Road to stable cut.
BULLECOURT	4/11/16	8.45am	Inspection by O.C. Gun drill and stoppages. Route march.	Work on camp proceeded with.

Map Reference

Army Form C. 2118.

WAR DIARY
or
INTELLIGENCE SUMMARY

(Erase heading not required.)

Instructions regarding War Diaries and Intelligence Summaries are contained in F. S. Regs., Part II. and the Staff Manual respectively. Title Pages will be prepared in manuscript.

Place	Date	Hour	Summary of Events and Information	Remarks and references to Appendices
MOYENNEVILLE	5/11/16		Heavy rain. Huts cleared out. Two hours spent on cleaning equipment	(Ilu)
	6/11/17		Limbers overhauled and cleaned. Brick paths laid in camp. Kitchen renovated. Stable roof tarred. Inside of stable whitewashed	(Ilu)
	7/11/17		Company paraded for Divisional G.O.Cs inspection. Postponed owing to rain. 2nd i/c and Section Officers inspected the line prior to relief on 8th.	(Ilu)
BULLECOURT S13 S.E.	8/11/17		Inter Company relief. 49 M.G.Coy relieved 48 M.G.Coy in Right Sector	(Ilu)
	9/11/17		Work in line carried on. No. 35 NEST position completed	(Ilu)
	10/11/17		5450 rds fired on TRIDENT TRENCH } in cooperation with raid by Infantry on our right 3750 " " SUNK RD (U11a) } Work carried on. Emplacements, dugouts etc improved	(Ilu)

MAP REFERENCE

Army Form C. 2118.

WAR DIARY
or
INTELLIGENCE SUMMARY

(Erase heading not required.)

Instructions regarding War Diaries and Intelligence Summaries are contained in F. S. Regs., Part II. and the Staff Manual respectively. Title Pages will be prepared in manuscript.

Place	Date	Hour	Summary of Events and Information	Remarks and references to Appendices
MOYENNEVILLE	11/11/17		3750 rds. fired on U15 c 00·05 3750 " " " U14 b 15·31 Situation very quiet	Ju
	12/11/17		1750 rds. fired on U21 c 20·80 1750 " " " U15 c 50·50 1000 " " " U21 a 80·40 In conjunction with gas bombardment	Ju
	13/11/17	7.30am	KNUCKLEAVE in vicinity of position 39 received attention with 4.2's QUEENSLANE also shelled with 4.2's Hostile M.G.s normal E.A. active during the afternoon Work carried on as usual	Ju 4·30 pm four 5·9sh close proximity to No 39 Position Work carried on
	14/11/17		2500 rds fired on U14 b 85·75 } in cooperation with T.M shoot 2500 rds " " U14 b 70·63 } Work carried on as usual Inter Company relief 48 M.G.Coy relieved 49 M.G.Coy in Right Sector " " 49 M.G.Coy " 48 M.G.Coy in Left Sector	Ju
BULLECOURT S18 S4y	15/11/17		Situation quiet	Ju

MAP REFERENCE

WAR DIARY or INTELLIGENCE SUMMARY

Army Form C. 2118.

Place	Date	Hour	Summary of Events and Information	Remarks and references to Appendices
MOYENNEVILLE	16/11/17		Situation very quiet. Work carried out on new barrage positions 80000 rds S.A.A. got up	Ebr
	17/11/17		8600 rds fired keeping enemy wire open in front of TUNNEL TRENCH 3500 rds fired on U2d 30.20 / U24b 48.25 1000 rds fired on white tape running from U14a 86.66 to U14b 30.20 Work carried on. 60000 rds S.A.A. got in (completing 210000 rds per gun)	Ebr
	18/11/17		8000 rds fired keeping enemy wire open in front of TUNNEL TRENCH 2500 rds fired on U2d 30.20 / U24b 43.25 1000 rds fired on white tape running from U14a 86.66 to U14b 30.20	Ebr
	19/11/17		Final preparations for barrage work. All guns overhauled Adequate supplies of oil, water etc got into positions	Ebr

BULLECOURT S/B SH.

Map Reference

WAR DIARY
or
INTELLIGENCE SUMMARY

(Erase heading not required.)

Army Form C. 2118.

Place	Date	Hour	Summary of Events and Information	Remarks and references to Appendices
MOEUVRES	20/11/17	6.20am	ATTACK on TUNNEL TRENCH and BOVIS TRENCH carried out by 16th Division and 3rd Division on our right. See operation orders attached. Rounds fired during Barrage { "No 8 Group" 92,000 / 50,000 / "R" Battery 30,000 } all guns No 8 Group. Rounds fired on S.O.S. (after consolidation) 140,000. Shoot on V 8d & V 15a 24,000 do. Shoot on OLDENBURG LANE 10,000 do. Shoot on FONTAINE LES CROISILLES 15,000 do. One O.R. killed. Five O.R. wounded. Wire of congratulation on barrage work and rapid engagement of targets received from H.Q. 9th Infantry Brigade.	Ap
BULLECOURT S.13.S.W.4.	21/11/17		Company relieved. Marched to MOYNE CAMP. Baths for men. Change of clean clothes.	Ap
	22/11/17		Cleaning guns - equipment etc. Afternoon Recreational training.	Ap
	23/11/17		C.O.'s inspection. Cleaning limbers. General overhaul.	Ap

Map Reference

WAR DIARY
INTELLIGENCE SUMMARY

Army Form C. 2118.

Place	Date	Hour	Summary of Events and Information	Remarks and references to Appendices
MOYENNEVILLE	24/11/17		Inspection by C.O. Full marching order. 2Lt. W. EASTON reported for duty. Physical Training	H.e
	25/11/17		Church Parades. Four lorries and Company taken to cinema shows at BÉHAGNIES.	H.e
S.E.13	26/11/17		Parades under Section Officers. 2LT C.S. SALMON attached from 2nd ROYAL IRISH REGIMENT for duty. Physical Training. Gas helmet drill	H.e
	27/11/17		Very wet. G.O.C.s inspection put off. 2LT N MURPHY attached from 7th R.I. REGT (S.I.H) for duty.	H.e
	28/11/17		A & M.G. Coy relieved A & M.G. Coy in LEFT SECTOR	H.e
BULLECOURT	29/11/17	5.30am	S.O.S. sent up by our troops. 37000 rds fired on S.O.S. lines. Casualties. J.D.R.	H.e
	30/11/17	5.50am	S.O.S. sent up on RIGHT SECTOR. Slow rate of fire maintained until situation became normal. 3250 rds fired	H.e

MAP REFERENCE

O.C. 49 M.G. Coy.

<u>SECRET.</u>

49ᵀᴴ MACHINE GUN COMPANY
OPERATION ORDER Nº 1   COPY Nº............

I. On a date to be notified later the 16ᵀᴴ Division will attack TUNNEL TRENCH and TUNNEL SUPPORT.

II. The following Machine Guns will be at the disposal of the 16ᵀᴴ Division.
    47 Machine Gun Coy ... 16
    48 " " " ... 16
    49 " " " ... 16
    34 Division 20

III. The above 68 guns will be used to produce covering and barrage fire and will be organised in batteries and groups of batteries.

IV. Groups will be numbered from RIGHT to LEFT.
Batteries will be lettered from RIGHT to LEFT.

V. The following will be the disposition of the 49ᵀᴴ M.G. Coy:-

Position	Group No.	Battery Letter	Section	No. of Guns
U.13.c.55.85.	8	P	'C'	4
U.13.c.45.95.	8	Q	'A'	4
T.6.b.15.90	9	R	'B'	4

'D' Section will form part of No. 7 Group and will be attached to the 48 M.G. Coy.

VI. Attached find appendix 'A' giving calculations, targets, etc. for the various batteries.

VII. <u>BARRAGE TIME TABLE.</u>
From Zero until Zero plus 30 minutes all guns allotted for covering and barrage fire will open fire on the above

barrage lines at the rate of 1 belt per minute. From Zero plus 30 minutes to Zero plus 1 hour, the rate will be one belt per two minutes, after which 1 belt per 5 minutes will be fired from Zero plus 1 hour to Zero plus 1 hour 30 minutes. After Zero plus 1 hour 30 minutes all barrage guns and teams will be held in readiness to open fire on their barrage lines in the event of:-
   (a) The enemy showing any increased activity with Artillery
   (b) S.O.S.

VIII(a) S.O.S. LINES.
   The barrage lines given in Appendix 'A' will be S.O.S. lines on which guns will fire after objectives have been captured.

VIII(b)   The following guns will however keep up intermittent fire on the following Secondary targets from Zero plus 2 hours until daybreak on Z plus 1 day, provided it is clearly understood that these are only Secondary tasks and that all guns are prepared to fire on S.O.S lines if required to do so.

IX   Attached appendix 'B' giving calculations, guns, and secondary targets.

X   The following stores will be at each gun position:-
     25 Boxes of S.A.A.
     14 Belt boxes
     1 Belt filling machine per two guns.
   One 4 gallon tin of water.
     1 Bottle oil.
     2 gallons of oil per battery
   Quantity of 4x2. (Flannelette)
     1 Spare barrel per gun.

VI. Group commanders will be under the control of the D.M.G.O. who will be located during active operations at 49 Inf. Bde H.Q. THE CAVES, CROISILLES.

VII. Group commanders will be prepared, with the assistance of a Fighting Map, to concentrate their fire on any given point at short notice. Locations of any enemy concentration will be notified by the D.M.G.O.

XIV. Each Section will be reinforced by six men from the infantry; these men should be instructed in belt filling, and can be used for carrying ammunition, etc.

XV. The following will be the location of the various H.Q's

49 M.G Coy H.Q.	ST LEGER.
Group commander No 7 Group	FACTORY.
" " " 8 "	QUARRY.
" " " 9 "	SHAFT 93 (SHAFT TRENCH)
D.M.G.O	CROISILLES (CAVES) WITH 49TH INF. BDE. H.Q.
48 Infantry Brigade	CROISILLES (CAVES)
47 " "	RAILWAY RESERVE.
49 " "	CROISILLES (CAVES)

Battalions of 49TH INF. BDE. as under

Right Battalion	U.7. d. 15.20.
Left "	U.7. d. 05.85.
Support "	T.22. d. 20.90.
Battalion holding line	T.6. b. 30.00 (SHAFT TRENCH).

18/4/17

_____
O.C. 49 M.G. Co.

APPENDIX "A"

GROUP No. 8

Battery Letter	Gun No.	Map Ref. of gun	Map Ref. Target	Range	True Bearing	V.I.	Q.E.
"P"	1	U13c 56·83	U8d 40·60	1650ˣ	58°	-3ᵐ	2°·35'
	2		U8d 34·70	"	56°	-4ᵐ	"
	3	U13c 53·86	U8d 28·80	"	55°	-6ᵐ	"
	4		U8d 22·90	"	53°	-7ᵐ	"
"Q"	1	U13c 49·95	U8d 18·98	1670ˣ	53°	-7ᵐ	2°·35'
	2		U8b 15·02	"	52°	-7ᵐ	2°·35'
	3	U13c 45·96	U8b 10·07	1700ˣ	51°	-8ᵐ	2°·45'
	4		U8b 10·13	"	50°	-8ᵐ	2°·45'

GROUP No. 9

Battery	Gun	Map Ref. of gun	Map Ref. Target	Range	True Bearing	V.I.	Q.E.
R	1	T6b 14·58	U8b 03·25	2275ˣ	121°	-25ᵐ	5°·10'
	2	T6b 16·60	U8a 95·30	2225ˣ	"	-26ᵐ	4°·50'
	3	T6b 18·60	U8a 87·38	2150ˣ	"	-27ᵐ	4°·20'
	4	T6b 20·62	U8a 80·45	2100ˣ	"	-27ᵐ	4°

APPENDIX "B"   Secondary Targets.

GROUP	BATTERY	Gun No.	Map ref. of gun	Map ref. of Target	Range	True Bearing	V.I.	Q.E.	Clearance
8	Q	3	U13c 45·96	U8b 35·25	1825ˣ	51°	-7ᵐ	3°·10'	16ˣ
		4		U8a 58·38	1600ˣ	41°	-8ᵐ	2°·15'	29ˣ
9	R	1	T6b 14·58	U8a 87·37	1950ˣ	124½°	-23ᵐ	3°·20'	51ˣ
		2	T6b 16·60	U8c 80·97	2250ˣ	125½°	-25ᵐ	5°	80ˣ

WAR DIARY,

FOR MONTH OF DECEMBER, 1917.

VOLUME :- 21

UNIT :- 119th Machine Gun Company. M.G.C.

Vol 20

CONFIDENTIAL.

WAR DIARY

OF THE

49th MACHINE GUN COY.

FOR

DECEMBER 1917.

WAR DIARY or INTELLIGENCE SUMMARY

Army Form C. 2118.

Place	Date	Hour	Summary of Events and Information	Remarks and references to Appendices
MOYENNEVILLE	1/12/17	night	Situation very quiet. Slow rate of fire maintained on S.O.S. lines during the night. 3000 rds. fired.	—
	2/12/17		4 M.G. Coy relieved in left sector by 121 M.G. Coy. Relief completed 3pm. Marched to MOYNE CAMP on completion of relief.	—
	3/12/17		Marched to BARASTRE AREA. Arrived 4pm.	—
	4/12/17		Stayed at BARASTRE.	—
	5/12/17		Marched to TINCOURT. Arrived 5pm.	—
	6/12/17		Embussed at HAMEL and moved to STE EMILIE. Arrived 1pm. Relieved 164 M.G. Coy, 169 M.G. Coy and 48 M.G. Coy. Relief complete 12.45 am 7/12/17.	—
	7/12/17		Situation quiet. No firing done.	—
	8/12/17		Situation quiet. Did not fire. Work started on the line. Emplacements, dugouts etc.	21HC
	9/12/17		Situation normal. Did not fire. 4 emplacements built.	21HC
	10/12/17		Situation normal. Enemy Artillery very active. Work continued on emplacements.	21HC
	11/12/17		Situation quiet, day being dull. Work progressing on emplacements.	21HC
	12/12/17		Situation normal. Heavy shelling of battery position by enemy.	21HC
	13/12/17		Situation normal. Enemy artillery fairly active.	21HC

Map ref BULLECOURT 51BSW.4

Map ref Sheet 57C 1/40,000

Map ref Sheet 62C 1/40,000

WAR DIARY
or
INTELLIGENCE SUMMARY.

Army Form C. 2118.

Place: EPEHY
Map Ref SHEET 62c 1/40,000 1/10,000

Date	Hour	Summary of Events and Information	Remarks and references to Appendices
14/12/17		Hostile Artillery very active MALASSISE TRE shelled. Our M. gun fired 4000 rounds.	S.H.C
15/12/17		Hostile Artillery again active. X 27 a swept by our guns during night. Works parties harrassed.	S.H.C
16/12/17		Situation normal. Our guns fired 4000 rounds on roads & tracks.	T.H.C
17/12/17		Situation normal. The usual harrassing fire was carried out.	T.H.C
18/12/17		Enemy artillery quiet during day. Enemy M. guns active during night. Our fire 450 rounds.	T.H.C
19/12/17		Enemy artillery normal. Our guns fired the usual harrassing fire.	T.H.C
20/12/17		Situation normal. Our M. guns fired 4000 rounds on A1 D7 & A10	T.H.C
21/12/17		Enemy artillery normal during day, fairly active during the evening.	T.H.C
22/12/17		Relieved by 47 M.G. Coy. relief complete by 6.30 p.m. Coy resting at Tin Court.	T.H.C
23/12/17		Cleaning up guns etc at Tin Court	T.H.C
24/12/17		At Tin Court	T.H.C
25/12/17		Xmas day spent at Tin Court	T.H.C
26/12/17		Preparing for the trenches	T.H.C
27/12/17		Relieved 48 M.G. Coy. relief complete at 6.u.r. Night passed normally.	T.H.C
28/12/17		Enemy Artillery active vicinity of St EMILIE fairly shelled. Our M.G. fired 2,500 rounds on A 20 c 00.45.	T.H.C

WAR DIARY or INTELLIGENCE SUMMARY.

Army Form C. 2118.

Place	Date	Hour	Summary of Events and Information	Remarks and references to Appendices
ST EMELIE	29/1/17		Enemy artillery active round ST EMELIE. Shelled with 15cm & 1.7cm. Their own M.guns fired 2050 rounds on cross roads A 20 c 0 D.4.5.	28 C
	30/1/17		Enemy artillery active. Enemy H.g.s active nearby QUEDGHEETE wood. Our M.guns fired 2050 rounds on A 20 C 09.45.	28 C
	31/1/17		Enemy artillery normal. His M.g.s active again. Own guns fired 2500 rounds on A 20 C 00 45.	29 C

Signed M. Mooney /.
O.C. 49 M.G. Co.

Map Ref
SHEET 62C
1/40 000

EPHEY
1:10,000

WAR DIARY,

FOR MONTH OF JANUARY, 1918.

VOLUME : 22

UNIT :- 49th Machine Gun Company
M.G.C.

Army Form C. 2118.

WAR DIARY
or
INTELLIGENCE SUMMARY.
(Erase heading not required.)

CONFIDENTIAL

WAR DIARY
OF THE
49TH MACHINE GUN COMPANY
FOR
JANUARY 1918.

Army Form C. 2118.

WAR DIARY
or
INTELLIGENCE SUMMARY

(Erase heading not required.)

Instructions regarding War Diaries and Intelligence Summaries are contained in F. S. Regs., Part II. and the Staff Manual respectively. Title pages will be prepared in manuscript.

Place	Date	Hour	Summary of Events and Information	Remarks and references to Appendices
ST. EMELIE.	1/1/18		**Artillery.** Hostile. Inactive during day, fairly active during night in RONSSOY & EPHEY. **Machine Guns** Hostile Machine Guns active during night. Guns fired 4000 rounds on the following targets:- 3000 rounds on A20c.00.45. 2000 " " A1d.40.40 2000 " " A1d.50.55 **Work.** New emplacements commenced at F22b.60.40, F22b.15.55, F15d.65.30, F17a.30.15 and 30.25	
	2/1/18		**Artillery.** Hostile. Very active throughout the day and night in RONSSOY & EPHEY. **Machine Guns** 8000 enemy Machine Guns active during night on forward roads and tracks. Guns fired 8000 rounds on the following targets:- 3000 rounds on A1d.40.40 3000 " " A1d.50.50 2000 " " A20c.00.45	
		4.30 am	At 4.30 am a heavy Artillery barrage was put down on our front line. Our Machine Guns opened at slow rate on S.O.S. lines. No hostile Infantry action followed.	
	3/1/18		**Artillery.** Hostile. Inactive. **Machine Guns** Enemy machine guns were active during night on tracks in the forward area. Guns fired 4000 rounds on special targets.	
	4/1/18		**Artillery.** Hostile. Daily active throughout the day in ST EMELIE, LEMPIRE, RONSSOY, and roads. Quiet during night. **Machine Guns** Enemy guns inactive during night. Guns fired 4500 rounds on the following targets: — 2500 rounds on BONY AVENUE A14.c.60.23 2000 " " Junction of Trench & A20c.30.75	

EPHEY
1:10,000

LEMPIRE
Special Sheet
1/10,000

(A7091). Wt. W12891/M1293. 753,000. 4/17. D. D. & L., Ltd. Forms/C.2118.14.

WAR DIARY
or
INTELLIGENCE SUMMARY

Army Form C. 2118.

Place	Date	Hour	Summary of Events and Information	Remarks and references to Appendices
ST EMELIE	1918 5 pm		Artillery. Hostile. Inaction during day. About 30 4.1 MMs were fired in forward area BASSE BOULOGNE. During activity during night.	
			Machine Guns. Hostile Machine Guns were active during night on the forward area. Guns fired 10,000 rounds on tracks in the following targets. 4000 rounds on 2000 yards point on BONY AVENUE A14c 60 23 2000 " " Junction of road and finish at A20c 30 75	
	6/7 Jan		Artillery. Hostile. Inaction during day.	
			Machine Guns. Hostile machine guns inactive. Guns fired 5000 rounds on the following targets. 3000 rounds fired on BONY AVENUE A14c 60 23 & Junction of road & finish at JA20c 30 75 2000 " "	
			Work. Revetting and improving emplacements. Operations at sub. H. Qrs. A.A. and splinter proof shelter. Guns & units improved. Communication night in forward areas. Junction.	
	4/5 pm		Artillery. Hostile. Daily active during night day.	
			Machine Guns. Hostile machine guns active during night on forward and rear fire. Guns and tracks on the following targets. 4000 rounds 2000 rounds at BONY AVENUE A14c 60 23 2000 " Junction of road and finish A20c 30 75	
			Work. Improving dugouts and emplacements. Guns fired and neutral.	

Army Form C. 2118.

WAR DIARY
or
INTELLIGENCE SUMMARY
(Erase heading not required.)

Instructions regarding War Diaries and Intelligence Summaries are contained in F.S. Regs., Part II. and the Staff Manual respectively. Title pages will be prepared in manuscript.

Place	Date	Hour	Summary of Events and Information	Remarks and references to Appendices
ST. EMELIE	1918 Aug 8		**Artillery.** Hostile Dairy active during day. Eny active during night in RONSSOY. About 30 H.E. 2 and 5.9 fired at BASSE BOULOGNE.	
			Machine guns. Hostile Machine guns were active on roads and tracks in the forward area. Guns fired 4,500 rounds on the following targets. 2500 fired at BONY AVENUE A14 c 60.23 2000 " " " " Junction of road and River at A20 c 30.45	
			Work. New emplacements dug. Minor dugouts improved.	
	Aug 9		**Artillery.** Hostile Dairy quiet by day, rather active during night in the vicinity of BASSE BOULOGNE, RONSSOY.	
			Machine guns. Enemy machine guns inactive. Guns fired 4500 rounds on the following targets:- 2000 on BONY AVENUE 2500 " A20 c 30.45	
			Work. Construction of new Section H.Q's. Work continued on incinerators of mens' dugout. & Funk hole between 9 + 10 positions. Ammunition shelter finished.	
	Aug 10		**Artillery.** Hostile Artillery very active throughout the night on the left. Especially between the hours 8.45 P.M. to 9.30 P.M. + 6.10 am to 6.45 am.	
			Machine Guns. Hostile Machine guns active on tracks and road in the forward area. Guns fired 3,500	

E P 44 1
1/10,000

LEMPIRE Special Sheet
1/10,000

WAR DIARY
or
INTELLIGENCE SUMMARY.
(Erase heading not required.)

Army Form C. 2118.

Instructions regarding War Diaries and Intelligence Summaries are contained in F. S. Regs., Part II. and the Staff Manual respectively. Title pages will be prepared in manuscript.

Place	Date	Hour	Summary of Events and Information	Remarks and references to Appendices
ST. EMELIE	1918 Jan 10		Rounds on the following targets:- 1500 rounds on A.20.c.30.75 of 2000 " " A.20c.30.75 of 2500 " " A.14.c.60.23. BONY AVENUE.	
	Jan 11		Work. Construction of dugout for 9 & 10 Sections continued. Construction of new Sect. H.Qrs. emplacements improved and revetted.	
			Artillery. Hostile Artillery inactive throughout the day. The Company was relieved in the line by the 4.4th Machine Gun Company. Relief complete at 5.45 p.m. On completion of relief the Company marched to ST EMELIE where they entrained for rest billets at TINCOURT, arriving at Billets at about 8.15 p.m.	
	Jan 12		Rest billets as per schedule attached.	
TINCOURT	Jan 13		A & B Sections proceeded to the Reserve trenches and built Eight emplacements as under:—	
62.C 1:40,000			Nos. S.1. F.21.c.09.66 — T piece, Sandbag platform and revetted. S.2. F.20.d.93.50 — T piece, Sandbag platform and revetted. Trench built to chany S.3. F.20.d.87.40 — T piece, Sandbag platform and revetted. Trench built to chany emplacement. S.4. F.26.b.30.90 — emplacement built. T piece, Sandbag platform and revetted, Trench built to chain emplacement.	

Army Form C. 2118.

WAR DIARY
or
INTELLIGENCE SUMMARY

(Erase heading not required.)

Instructions regarding War Diaries and Intelligence Summaries are contained in F. S. Regs., Part II. and the Staff Manual respectively. Title pages will be prepared in manuscript.

Place	Date	Hour	Summary of Events and Information	Remarks and references to Appendices
TINCOURT	1918 Nov. 3rd Jan 13		S7. F26a 68.32. Emplacement built. T piece, Sandbag platform. S8. F26a 75.20 Emplacement built, T piece, Sandbag platform. S9. F25d 66.24 } S10. F25d 67.14 } Emplacement built, T piece, Sandbags platforms. Trench connecting these emplacements not quite completed and revetting to finish.	
			Dumps F20d 88.48 This dump contains 20000 S.A.A. Built of bags. elephants and revetted at back and sides. This dump supplies 1, 2, 3, & 4 positions.	
			F26b 69.25 This dump containing 10000 S.A.A. is built of baby elephants and is revetted at back and sides. It supplies 7 & 8 positions. This dump has a trench to drain it.	
			F25d 66.24 This dump contains 10000 S.A.A. Similar to others. This dump supplies 9 & 10 gun positions.	
			At 4.30 p.m. the above two Sections entrained at TEMPLEUX LE GUERARD arriving at Rest Billets, TINCOURT at about 5.30 p.m.	
	Jan 14th		C & D Sections proceeded by train to Risian River following days. Emplacements and Dumps.	
			No. B2 F25c 89.92. Emplacement dug. Trench dug. B3 F25a 90.50 Emplacement dug. T piece. Emplacement revetted. One strip duck boarded.	

WAR DIARY
or
INTELLIGENCE SUMMARY.

(Erase heading not required.)

Army Form C. 2118.

Place	Date	Hour	Summary of Events and Information	Remarks and references to Appendices
TINCOURT.	1918. Jan 14th		B4 F25b 00.70 — Emplacement built, T piece, Emplacement revetted. Our S.A.P Duck boarded.	
	15th		B5 F19a 10.45 Emplacement built, Sand bag platform, Emplacement revetted. Recess for S.A.A built & 5000 S.A.A deposited. Trench Duck boarded.	
	16th		B6 F19b 20.80 Emplacement built. Sand bag platform. Revetted. Recess for S.A.A built and 5000 S.A.A deposited. Trench Duck boarded.	
	17th		Dump E25a 98.63 This dump contains 10000 S.A.A. It is built of heavy elephants and is revetted at back and sides. No supply B2, 3 & 4 positions.	
	18th		The above two sections returned at TEMPLEUX LE GUERARD, arriving back in rest billets at about 4 p.m.	
	19		Company parades as per Schedule attacked. Company parades as per Schedule attacked. Company parades as per Schedule attacked. Company parades as per Schedule attacked. Company parades as per Schedule attacked.	
STEMELIE	20		The 49th M.G.C. relieved the 48th M.G.C. in the left Sector in the line. The Company left Rest Billets TINCOURT by bus Marched to 2.30 p.m. arriving at ST. EMELIE at about 4.30 p.m. M.T. Lim Relief Complete at 6.15 p.m. Night fairly quiet. Enemy Machine guns inactive. Artillery fairly active in EPEHY.	

Ad 2A
EPEHY 1/10000
LE PIPRE Special Sht. 1/10000
STEMELIE 1/10000

WAR DIARY
INTELLIGENCE SUMMARY

Army Form C. 2118.

Place	Date	Hour	Summary of Events and Information	Remarks and references to Appendices
ST EMELIE	1918 Jan 21		**Situation** Quiet. **Artillery.** Hostile Artillery quiet during day, fairly active throughout the night. **Machine Guns** Quiet. **Work.** Improving dugouts and emplacements. Construction of shafts under Sappers.	
	Jan 22		**Artillery.** Hostile Artillery active throughout the day, especially in ST. EMELIE. ST. EMELIE was heavily shelled with 5.9 and gas shells between 2.30 pm and 6 pm. No casualties. Cloud 18 long N₂h₃. **Machine Guns.** Hostile Mus.M.Gs. very active throughout the night in forward area. **Work.** Construction of shafts under R.E. Sappers. Trench revetted, dugout improved, emplacements revetted.	
	Jan 23		**Artillery.** Hostile Artillery very active in EPEHY between 9am & 11.30am to Sch. Mks. in Railway cutting. No casualties. **Machine Guns.** Hostile Mus.M.Gs. inactive. **Work.** Shafts continued, shafts at 29 Q.P. revetted. No 32 gun position built. Revetting trench at new position & Lewis gun position built where pullin in.	

EPEHY Special Sheet 1:10,000

LEMPIRE Special Sheet 1:10,000

Army Form C. 2118.

WAR DIARY
or
INTELLIGENCE SUMMARY.
(Erase heading not required.)

CONFIDENTIAL

WAR DIARY

OF

49TH MACHINE GUN COMPANY

FOR

MONTH OF FEBRUARY 1918

WAR DIARY or INTELLIGENCE SUMMARY

Army Form C. 2118.

Place	Date	Hour	Summary of Events and Information	Remarks and references to Appendices
TINCOURT	1/2/18		Coy resting - Drills at Tincourt. Training as per programme attached	WC
	2/2/18	6.30		
	2/2/18		Coy relieved 269 M.G. Coy in the right sector. Relief completed by 6.30 p.m. The night passed quietly. Our machine guns fired 2000 rounds at dugouts & tracks in vicinity at A.8.c. 45.48	WC
	3/2/18		Artillery on both sides quiet owing to dull weather. Harassing fire continued on A.8.c 45.48. 2000 rounds being fired. Emplacements rebuilt & a mine shaft at F23.c 95.10 continued with.	WC
ST EMILIE	4/2/18		Hostile artillery showed considerable activity. A battery fired two in RONSSOY at F21.B.30.20. Heavily shelled three times during the day. During the afternoon LEMPIRE received attention with 4.2's. Fairly calm about F.16 a 90.80. Enemy M.G.s active throughout the night. Ours fired 1500 rounds at an E.A. West flew over our lines about 4.30 p.m. 2000 rounds at A.8.C 45.48. Work continued on the mine shaft F23c.90.10	WC

Ref. Maps SHEET 62cNE 2.
Special shut. pash of 57c SE 57B S.W. 62C NE
and 62 B N.W.

Army Form C. 2118.

WAR DIARY
or
INTELLIGENCE SUMMARY.
(Erase heading not required.)

Instructions regarding War Diaries and Intelligence Summaries are contained in F.S. Regs., Part II. and the Staff Manual respectively. Title pages will be prepared in manuscript.

Place	Date	Hour	Summary of Events and Information	Remarks and references to Appendices
ST ENELIE	10/2/18		Hostile artillery again active from the direction of BONY. LEMPIRE again received attention from 4.25 & high bursting shrapnel. About 5 pm the enemy commenced to bombard the left of the Division on our right & the S.O.S. was seen. There from covering the front opened fire & 2000 rounds were expended. A 8 c 45. 48. received 1000 rounds & A 14.D. 0V 20 1000 also. Enemy M.G.s active throughout the night.	2HC
	11/2/18 2km		Both hostile & our artillery fairly active during the day. Tracks round BONY Ave Swept with fire with front line observation. Many Germans observed & some were seen to take cover hurriedly. This area was swept during the night. Total ammunition expended 3000 rounds. Many of the enemy were observed round the Quarry at A14B 9.0 97. the enemy were observed round the Quarry 2000 rounds fired. was engaged during the night. 2000 rounds fired. Hostile M.G.s active throughout the night.	2HC
	12/2/18		Both artilleries quiet during the day. the enemy who could be observed again engaged a few of the enemy who could be observed 2000 rounds fired. A7 D 58.55 & vicinity received 1500 rounds during the night. BONY Ave & trenches 2500 rounds. Quarry & tracks A14 B 90. 97. during afternoon & night 3000 rounds.	2HC

WAR DIARY or INTELLIGENCE SUMMARY

Army Form C. 2118.

(Erase heading not required.)

Place	Date	Hour	Summary of Events and Information	Remarks and references to Appendices
ST ELIE	13/2/18		Hostile artillery action rather heavy at 5 pm. "Gap at ref." Ronssoy heavily shelled at this hour. Our machine guns carried out retaliatory harassing shoots during the night. BONY AVENUE + tracks in the vicinity received 2500 rounds. A 14 C 85.77 "2000 rounds + QUENNEMONT FARM 2500 rounds.	WC
	14/2/18		Hostile Artillery normal. Our machine guns carried out the following harassing fire. BONY AVE + tracks 2000 rounds A 14 C 85.77 2000 rounds QUENNEMONT FARM 2500 rounds	WC
	16/2/18		Hostile artillery action in retaliation to ours. QUEUCHETTE WOOD shelled with 5.9's + 8"s in the late afternoon. Our machine guns fired during the night on the following targets QUENNEMONT FARM 2000 rounds. BONY AVE 1500 rounds. Quarry at A 14 B 90 85 2000.	WC

Army Form C. 2118.

WAR DIARY
or
INTELLIGENCE SUMMARY.
(Erase heading not required.)

Instructions regarding War Diaries and Intelligence Summaries are contained in F. S. Regs., Part II. and the Staff Manual respectively. Title pages will be prepared in manuscript.

Place	Date	Hour	Summary of Events and Information	Remarks and references to Appendices
	17/2/18		Enemy artillery active during the day. Front line shelled & F.15.a Central & area in vicinity heavily shelled with 5.9s a few fell in Ronssoy about F.21.3 50.20. Our artillery was very active cutting wire & on back areas. During the night our machine guns fired on gaps in the wire at the following points. TARGET — ROUNDS FIRED A.13.B.70.99 — 1000 A.7.D.35.70 — 1250 A.20.a.00.70 — 1000 A.13.D.40.60 — 1000 A.14.C.90.80 — 2000	[signature]
	18/2/18		Enemy artillery normal. Ronssoy lightly shelled during 8.15 9.15 — As soon as the patrols came in our guns fired on gaps in the wire. All preparation ready for the raid.	[signature]

Army Form C. 2118.

WAR DIARY
or
INTELLIGENCE SUMMARY.

(Erase heading not required.)

Instructions regarding War Diaries and Intelligence Summaries are contained in F. S. Regs., Part II. and the Staff Manual respectively. Title pages will be prepared in manuscript.

Place	Date	Hour	Summary of Events and Information	Remarks and references to Appendices
STEENLIE	1918 Jan 24		Artillery. Hostile fairly quiet, EPEHY was shelled in the forenoon with 5.9.	
			Machine Guns. Hostile very active during night on forward roads and tracks.	
			Work. Shafts at 29 position revetted & emplacement. Re-erecting shelter next tubes. New emplacements completed for guns 2,3. Sandbagged platform & trench revetting. Sap revetted and Arch tunnel.	
			The 29th M.G.C. (New Bvr. Corps) joined us in the line for instruction for 4 days.	
	25 4.40 am		Artillery. Hostile fairly quiet during day and night. At about 4.30 am, enemy artillery was very active till about 5.30 am. S.O.S. was upshot no hostile infantry action followed.	
			Machine guns. Hostile fairly active throughout the night. In rounds & tracks in the forward area. Guns fired 13000 rounds at slow rate on S.O.S. lines. 2000 rounds fired on KILDARE POST. 2000 rounds fired on HOLT'S BANK.	
			Work. Emplacement at No 21 gun finished. Splinter proof at No R6 position built. At No 24 position ammunition recess built. Work in all dug-outs continued.	

WAR DIARY
or
INTELLIGENCE SUMMARY

Army Form C. 2118.

Place	Date	Hour	Summary of Events and Information	Remarks and references to Appendices
ST EMELIE	1918 Jan 26		**Artillery** Hostile Artillery fairly active throughout the day in EPHEY ST EMELIE. Quiet during night.	
			Machine Guns Hostile active throughout the night on roads and tracks in forward area. Bursts fired 4000 rounds on 3 special targets. 2000 fired on KILDARE POST, 2000 rounds fired on HOLTS BANK.	
			Work. Construction of shafts under R.E. sappers. New position built at YAK POST.	
	27th		**Artillery** Hostile inactive during day and night.	
			Machine Guns Hostile inactive. Bursts fired 8000 rounds on 3 special targets. 1500 fired on KILDARE POST, 1500 rounds fired on HOLTS BANK.	
			Work. Emplacement at No 21 position raised 18 ft. New water and picket line built. New lines constructed. New hut filling shelters built at No 25 & 26 positions. Shafts continued under R.E. sappers.	
	28th		**Artillery** Hostile normal.	
			Machine Guns Hostile inactive.	
			Work. Recess built for tell tales at No 21 gun position. New water and duck boarded. Construction of shafts under R.E. Sappers continued.	

EPHEY 1.10,000

LEMPIRE Special Sheet 1.10,000

Army Form C. 2118.

WAR DIARY
or
INTELLIGENCE SUMMARY
(Erase heading not required.)

Place	Date	Hour	Summary of Events and Information	Remarks and references to Appendices
ST. EMELIE	1918 Jan 29		**Artillery** Hostile Quiet. **Machine Guns** Hostile fairly active during the night on RAILWAY EMB. F.I.O. guns fired two rounds on special target, 2000 on HOLTS BANK, 2000 on KILDARE POST, 5000 rounds were fired at E.A. **Work.** Construction of shafts under R.E. Sappers. Races for hot loaves built at No 24 gun position.	
	30		**Artillery** Hostile very active in the vicinity of STE EMELIE, 8" being used. Wire in the forward area. The 48th M.G.C. relieved the 49th M.G.C. in the line at 6.30 pm. On completion of relief the relief party marched by gun crews to Hdqs STE EMELIE at 8 pm. The returned arriving at rest billets TINCOURT at about 9 pm.	
TINCOURT	31		Parades as per Schedule attached.	
LEHPIRE	Oct 1		Company as per Schedule attached.	

A/ Clymor lt
A/ O.C. 40 M.G. Co.

49th Machine Gun Coy Training Programme for Period Jan 13th to 18th 1918

Time	12th Jan	13th Jan	14th Jan	15th Jan	16th Jan	17th Jan	18th Jan
7.15am	Reveille	Reveille	Reveille	Reveille	Reveille	Reveille	Reveille
8.0 am	Breakfast	Breakfast	Breakfast	Breakfast	Breakfast	Breakfast	Breakfast
9.0 am to 9.30	C.O. Parade	C.O. Parade	C.O. Parade	C.O. Parade	C.O. Parade	C.O. Parade	C.O. Parade
9.30 to 10.30	Bath & Clothing			Operation of guns	Cleaning Limbers	Mechanism	Stoppages	Gun Drill
10.30 to		H and B Sections Burying Reserve Emplacements	C and D Sections Cleaning Guns	Lecture Map Reading	Route March	Lecture Map Reading Use of Compass	Route March
11.30		C and D Sections Burying Reserve Emplacements	H and B Sections Cleaning Guns	Break	Break	Break	Break
11.30 to 12.30				Drill Indian Section Officers	Infantry School Committee of Kit Bags	Instruction of Taking at Enemy Aircraft Range-Finder	
12.30 pm to 1.0 pm				Physical Training	Physical Training	Physical Training	Physical Training
1.15 pm to 2.0 pm							Packing for Line

Vol 22

WAR DIARY.

FOR MONTH OF FEBRUARY, 1918.

VOLUME:- 23

UNIT:- 49th Machine Gun Company

Army Form C. 2118.

WAR DIARY
or
INTELLIGENCE SUMMARY.

Place: ST EMELIE

Date	Hour	Summary of Events and Information	Remarks and references to Appendices
19/9/18	4 a.m.	This morning the 7th Bn. R. Munster Fus. carried out a raid on the enemy trenches at A.70.50.90 with the object of penetrating to A.S.A.00.80 on a front of 200 yards. Our machine gun Coop. arty. will the artillery fired for 40 min. on the following targets.	M.C

TARGET	ROUNDS FIRED
A.14.c.50.60	6250
C.T. in A.8.c	7000
Bony Ave	6000
A.14.c.10.25	6000
A.1.D.15.15	2500
A.1.D.20.30	2500
Maquincourt Trench A.2.c	12000
A.7.B.20.90	3000

The enemy fired many red lights which were answered about Zero + 5 by his artillery. Our casualties were hit & those of the raider slight whilst the enemys were heavy.

WAR DIARY
or
INTELLIGENCE SUMMARY

Army Form C. 2118.

Place	Date	Hour	Summary of Events and Information	Remarks and references to Appendices
ST EMELIE	20/2/18		Enemy put down a heavy barrage at 5.45 pm on the left of the 24th Division the barrage lasted for about 1 hour, then again put down the barrage from 8.30 to 9 pm. At 4.30 am 21/2/18 an attempted raid on the 39th Div on our left was repulsed. Our guns fired 7500 rounds on S.O.S. lines. 3000 rounds were fired during the night at Bony Ave & tracks in vicinity.	L/HQ
	21/2/18		Hostile artillery active during the morning & afternoon, Vicinity of F.15.A.30.70 shelled all morning with 4.2" shells. SANDBAG ALLEY shelled lightly will 4.2s during the afternoon. Our machine guns carried out harassing fire during the night BONY Ave & tracks 2080 rounds. Tracks A.14.c.80.70 2000. Hostile M.G.s fairly active.	L/HQ

Army Form C. 2118.

WAR DIARY
or
INTELLIGENCE SUMMARY.
(Erase heading not required.)

Place	Date	Hour	Summary of Events and Information	Remarks and references to Appendices
ST EMELIE	22/2/18	At 4.45 a.m. this morning there was a heavy bombardment on extreme left, nothing developed on our front. The vicinity of F.2.B.c.80.10 shelled with 4.2s. SART FARM lightly shelled with 77 m.m. Our H.G's fired 3000 rounds on roads & tracks round BONY AVE. Enemy M.G's fairly active.	M.C
	23/2/18		Hostile artillery fairly active. SANDBAG ALLEY shelled intermittently throughout the night. Our M.G's fired 2000 rounds on tracks round A.14.D.00.20. Hostile guns fairly active.	M.C
	24/2/18		Enemy artillery very active throughout the day. SANDBAG ALLEY shelled with about 30 5.9s. LEMPIRE EAST & CENTRAL shelled with 4.2s & a few gas shells. Our trench guns fired 1000 rounds on A.14.D.00.20 & 1500 rounds on QUENNEMONT FARM.	M.C

WAR DIARY
or
INTELLIGENCE SUMMARY.
(Erase heading not required.)

Army Form C. 2118.

Place	Date	Hour	Summary of Events and Information	Remarks and references to Appendices
ST EMELIE	25/2/18		Hostile artillery again fairly active. LEMPIRE RONSSOY SART FARM shelled with 77 mm ? 4.2's about 50 each. Vicinity of BASSE BOULOGNE shelled with 4.2's & few 5.9's. Our machine guns fired 2000 rounds on QUENNEMONT FARM & 1500 rounds on BONY AVE & tracks in vicinity.	JMC
	26/2/18		Enemy shelled RONSSOY with 5.9's during the afternoon a few gas shells in the valley F9.0. At 11.50 pm the enemy put down a heavy bombardment on our right on SOS machine guns fired 6000 rounds at slow rate on SOS lines. Situation became normal about 12.30 midnight.	JMC

Army Form C. 2118.

WAR DIARY
or
INTELLIGENCE SUMMARY.
(Erase heading not required.)

Place	Date	Hour	Summary of Events and Information	Remarks and references to Appendices
ST EMILIE	27/9/18		Coy relieved in the line by the 62nd Coy 21st Divs. Relief completed by 9 pm. Coy entrained & went into billets at TINCOURT.	
	28/9/18		Coy in Billets. TINCOURT.	

J M Collinson Lieut
for O.C. 49 M.G. Co.

TRAINING PROGRAMME 31·1·18 to 7·2·18 — 49th MACHINE GUN Coy.

HOUR.	THURSDAY.	FRIDAY.	SATURDAY.	SUNDAY	MONDAY.	TUESDAY.	WEDNESDAY.	THURSDAY.
8.45 a.m.	Section Officers' Parade		Section Officers' Parade		Section Officers' Parade	Section Officers' Parade	Section Officers' Parade	
9.0 a.m.	C.O.'s Parade.		C.O.'s Parade.	← CHURCH PARADE →	C.O.'s Parade.	C.O.'s Parade.	C.O.'s Parade.	CLEANING GUNS AND PREPARING FOR TRENCHES.
9.15 a.m.	Cleaning Guns	← BATHS →	Gun Drill.		Section Drill	Gun Drill from Limbers.	Gun Drill	
10.15 a.m.	Cleaning Limbers		Packing Limber Drill.		Lecture on "Attack and Defence"	Lecture on "Anti-Aircraft Range Taking Work"	Lecture on "Anti-Aircraft Range Taking"	
11.30 a.m. to 12.30 p.m.	Cleaning Camp.	Lecture on "Range Cards"	Physical Training.		Physical Training.	Physical Training.	Physical Training.	
AFTERNOON	Recreation.	Recreation.	Recreation.	Recreation	Recreation.	Recreation.	Recreation.	

1979/6

Brigade Trench Mortar Battery

Oct 1915 - Dec 1915

~~2 Antl Tmes~~
~~16 DIV 49 Bde~~

49

TRENCH MORTAR
BTY

1915 Oct to 1915 DEC

~~1692~~

Army Form. C. 2118

WAR DIARY
or
INTELLIGENCE SUMMARY 49th Trench Mortar Battery

(Erase heading not required.)

Instructions regarding War Diaries and Intelligence Summaries are contained in F. S. Regs., Part II. and the Staff Manual respectively. Title Pages will be prepared in manuscript.

Place	Date	Hour	Summary of Events and Information	Remarks and references to Appendices
BERTHEN	10.17		49th Trench Mortar Battery formed with 2 Lt. HAMILTON as Off. Comd'g. Rana Butler as 2.i.c. and proceed to 2.5 Div arty H.Q. at NIEPPE and report for orders. Allotted billets and proceed to make men comfortable.	
			Improving billets.	
NIEPPE	13		Received orders to relieve 30th T.M.B. at Ploeg St. Wood, west of Nunnay 15th.	
	14		Reconnoitre positions	
PLUG ST. WOOD	15		Took over advanced billets from 30th T.M.B. Placed guns in action. Zeroed 10 rounds at what appeared to be a dam in front of trench 123. Shot too round fell short & sentry large columns of water. Got 4 hits on trench but not at desired spot. Flan find one round well to left & one well to right so the Bombers likely affected from Zone of fire.	
			10 rounds fired at 3.45 p.m. at hour Shut 2 & hoist V.15 d 9.3. 1 dud. Good results.	

WAR DIARY
or
INTELLIGENCE SUMMARY

Army Form. C. 2118

Place	Date	Hour	Summary of Events and Information	Remarks and references to Appendices
PIVGST WOOD	18	4pm	Opened fire on smoke emerging from enemy trench at four points, one round at each. All four were rather close to objective. Owing to rain & mist could not say whether we did hits or not. Fired rounds more rapid at trench to left of smoke. Expect we did some damage as very heavy retaliation followed. Probables had 4 trench mortars going. As they were heavier than ours and considerably out-ranged us we ceased fire by request. No rounds fired. See print.	
	19			

J.P. Hamilton 2Lt R.G.A
Comdg 49 T. Mortar Bty

Army Form C. 2118

WAR DIARY
or
INTELLIGENCE SUMMARY

(Erase heading not required.) 118th French Mortar Battery, RFA Divison.

Instructions regarding War Diaries and Intelligence
Summaries are contained in F. S. Regs., Part II.
and the Staff Manual respectively. Title Pages
will be prepared in manuscript.

Place	Date	Hour	Summary of Events and Information	Remarks and references to Appendices
	25/9/15		Looked round + chose sites for gun emplacements.	
	26/9/15		Chose sites for dug outs + commenced work on gun emplacements	
	27/9/15		Gun emplacements finished, ready to mount guns into.	
	28/9/15		Capt. Calaghan took over Battery	

Ja Sh
R.A.M. McCook Capt
R.F.A. Mortar

1875 Wt. W593/826 1,000,000 4/15 J.B.C. & A. A.D.S.S./Forms/C. 2118.

WAR DIARY
or
INTELLIGENCE SUMMARY

(Erase heading not required.)

Army Form C. 2118

4th Bedford Mortar Battery

Place	Date	Hour	Summary of Events and Information	Remarks and references to Appendices
PLOEGSTEERT WOOD	Dec 10-12		Nothing doing	
	13	4 p.m.	Fired 8 rounds at enemy's front trench opposite T123 Reg 15. Fairly good result. We succeeded in our object which was to "put the wind up" the enemy.	
	14/15		Nothing doing	
	16th	3 p.m.	Fired 37 rounds at enemy fire trench with the object of damaging enemy's gas apparatus if there were any. Result 19 hits, 1 air burst, 1 short, 1 not burst & the remainder over.	
	17th	3.30 p.m.	Fired 35 rounds at enemy's fire trench, a continuation of yesterday's strafe. Result 16 hits, 2 air bursts, 2 short, 5 on parapet and the remainder over.	
LE GHEER	18-19		Preparing howitzers at LE GHEER.	
	20	4 p.m.	Opened fire in conjunction with 2" & 4" H.Y. T.M. B.ttys. Fired 82 rounds in all. We got about 40% hits, 30% on the wire & 30% over.	
PLOEGSTEERT WOOD	21-26		Preparing howitzers for strafing the BIRDCAGE.	

B.W.H. Smith? 2nd R.S.A.
O.C. 49 T.M.B.

www.ingramcontent.com/pod-product-compliance
Lightning Source LLC
Chambersburg PA
CBHW081410160426
43193CB00013B/2148